Weekly Rep
~ *a theatrical phenomenon* ~

Richard A. Jerrams

Peter Andrew Publishing
Company Limited

First edition 1991

Published by
PETER ANDREW PUBLISHING COMPANY LIMITED

ISBN 0 946796 43 2

Typeset in Great Britain by
Steven Graphics,
Droitwich, Worcestershire, England

Printed and bound in Great Britain

Contents

For Ann-Marie,
Laurence and Stephen

Foreword

I have been invited to write this foreword because I am a product of 'Weekly Rep' and, I may say proud to 'confess' it. During 50 years in the theatre I look back on my two seasons, of 45 weeks each, at the Little Theatre, Bristol, with nostalgia and in gratitude and loyalty. I cannot say I learned my job there – I am still learning it – but MY God! I learned to work. I find myself often today playing in some companies whose younger members have never entered a stage-door. For all their advantage of having been to drama school – an advantage I never enjoyed – there is a gap in their theatrical experience. This book is for them.

A book which fills a place in the history of our profession – a timely and loving reminder of a theatrical period gone for ever but here recaptured before it is too late. A reminder of the time between the days of the touring Actor-Manager – (change at Crewe on Sundays) and the advent of films and the television which knows no stage-door. A book too for those who sat the other side of the foot-lights (we had foot-lights in those days) to remind them of the seats they occupied every Tuesday or Saturday or whenever to follow, with loyal interest the careers of their favourites – the butler this week, the master next, Macbeth the week after. A book so well researched that there is little this writer can contribute. I wish he could add "Long live Weekly Rep" – but alas! he cannot, it has gone forever – except in such a book as this.

Sir Michael Hordern, C.B.E.

Acknowledgements

This book would not have been possible without the help of many contributors. I'm deeply grateful to the Librarians of the forty libraries, in towns between Plymouth and Dundee, whose response to my Questionnaire, with one or two exceptions, was indicative of good archive organisation. To the Editors of local newspapers, in towns throughout the British Isles, who published my letter requesting 'memories and impressions' of 'their Rep', and to the many theatregoers who responded – too many to mention all by name. To the Editor of the 'The Stage and Television Today' for publishing letters requesting information about Weekly Reps, and my thanks to all who replied.

To Colin Bean, Arthur Spreckley, Diana Glyn, Rex Howard-Arundel, John Bennett, Russell Morley, Joe Holroyd, Wilfred Harrison, Derek Salberg, CBE, and the late Joan Lowe for inviting me to their homes to record their observations on Weekly Rep, and theatre generally.

I am indebted to Joseph Wright, Prof. Emeritus of Drama at Vanderbilt University, Nashville, Tennessee; to Douglas Russell, Prof. of Drama at Stanford University, California; Roy Gentry, and Bryan Douglas, for their comments on Tom Osborne Robinson.

Had I begun my research in 1992, rather than, as was the case, in 1982, I would have missed the encouragement and valuable contributions of the late J. C. Trewin, Richard Leacroft, John Haerem, C.B.E., Joseph Walker, Joan Lowe, David Manderson, Aubrey Dyas, Lou Warwick , Russell Morley, and Geoffrey Wood. I honour their memory.

My thanks to Gay Rogers for the efficient typing of my text: Ian Hunter for valuable help with the Illustrations: to Judith Ann Walker for help with the Index.

I am grateful to the following publishers, and others, for permission to quote from copyright material.

Methuen, London: Just Resting, Leo McKern, 1984.
Phaidon Press Ltd: Theatre – A Personal View, Harold Hobson, 1984.
William Collins: Autobiography, Neville Cardus, 1947.
Arlington Books Publishers Ltd: All My Burning Bridges, Pat Phoenix, 1974.
The Bodley Head: Old and Young, Ivor Brown, 1971.

Harrap Ltd: The Selective Ego, edited by T. Beaumont, 1976.
The Athlone Press: From Irving to Olivier, Michael Sanderson, 1984.
Faber & Faber Ltd: Subsequent Performances, Jonathan Miller, 1986.
A Better Class of Person, John Osborne, 1981.
Changeable Scenery, Richard Southern, 1952.
Columbus Books (W. H. Allen): A Life in the Theatre, Tyrone Gurthrie, 1988.
Bristol Classical Press: The Arts in a State, John Pick, 1988.
Hamish Hamilton Ltd: Young Gemini, Alec McCowen, 1979,
Jonathan Cape: The Theatres of George Devine, Irving Wardle, 1978.
Martin Secker and Warburg: Sir Donald Woolfit, Ronald Harwood, 1971.
Basil Blackwell: Philosophical Investigations, Ludwig Wittgenstein, 1967.
Cambridge University Press: The Repertory Movement, G. Rowell & A
Jackson, 1984.
David Higham Associates Ltd: The Play and the Audience, L. Macniece,
One Man in His Time, Bruce Belfrage, 1951.
Curtis Brown and John Farquharson: Master of One, Dorian Williams, 1978.
David Bonnar, General Manager Perth Repertory Theatre, from the Theatre in
Perth by Roy Boutcher & William Kemp, and Perth Theatre 1935--1985.
James Carter: Oldham Coliseum Theatre – The First Hundred Years, 1986.
Jane Greaves: Oldham Theatres.
York Central Library: The York Theatre Royal, Sybil Rosenfeld, 1948.
D. Elleray, A.L.A.,F.R.S.A., Worthing Theatres, 1970-1984, 1985.
The Guardian: Article by Robin Thorber, June 1st, 1985.
The Chronicle and Echo, Northampton: Extract from letter published
22.12.75.
Times Newspapers Ltd: From reviews by James Agate, 1941 and John Peter,
1984.
Ronald Russell: The Story of the Little Theatre, Bristol, 1948.
Simon Callow, for the extract from his review of Rex Harrison by Roy Moseley.
Derek Salberg: My Love Affair with a Theatre, 1978.

My thanks to the following for permission to use the photographs numbered: Colin Bean (2.1); Helen Leacroft (2.5-6);
Bryan Douglas (5.1); Ronald Russell (7.1-4); Derek Salberg
(9.1-2); Kay Gosnell (9.3); Reed Northern Newspapers (Yorkshire) Ltd. (15.1-2); Mary Kinloch Parker (19.1-3); Stanley Wild
(19.4, 21.1).

The author has made every effort to trace the owners of
copyright material that appears in this book and wishes to
acknowledge the copyright of any material where its source has
not been traced.

I am deeply indebted to Philip and Joan Checkley of Peter
Andrew Publishing Company Limited for making the book
possible, and their careful editing of the text. The author is
solely responsible for the opinions expressed.

Finally, my heartfelt thanks to Sir Michael Hordern, C.B.E. for
his generous foreword.

List of Illustrations

"Theatre, like life, is not about continuous successes; but about wonderful moments that make all the rest seem worthwhile. . "

Maurice Browne....

who made a fortune from his production of 'Journey's End', and lost it all financing theatrical enterprises – to a company of which the author was a member.

The most beautiful actress in the country, robed as a medieval queen by a superb designer, who has also done a wonderful set, may offer us a death scene in which she speaks the most sumptuous rhetoric, accompanied by music supplied by one of our best composers; and yet we may feel nothing at all; whereas, at a neighbouring theatre, against a dingy commonplace setting, a rather ugly young woman in a dirty mackintosh may mutter an apparently banal phrase or two, and yet make us feel all the heartbreak of this life and so haunt our imagination for years. In the first theatre we have been offered all the trappings and nothing else, and in the second theatre we have experienced the peculiar art of drama. And its wonder and its beauty are all its own, and must not be confused with other kinds.

J. B. Priestley

Introduction

To the question, "What does Weekly Rep mean to you?", which I put to young and old persons during my six years of researching this subject, I have received varied answers. In the main, from the under 20's, the response has often been one of bewilderment, and questions such as "Do you mean some kind of a salesman who calls every week, like the Bettaware rep?"

The slightly older age group, by which I mean 30/40ish, responded in a way that indicated that they knew it was some kind of theatrical activity. "Oh you mean all that ad-libbing and busking that went on" was the reply I had from quite a few people.

Older people would often display a strong mood of nostalgia, which has been repeated by correspondents replying to letters requesting 'memories and impressions' of 'their rep', which I have had published in the letters columns of local papers from Hastings and Plymouth in the south to Dundee in the north. I found that even people who worked in Weekly Rep companies were surprised to find that its extent was as broad geographically; and its duration, historically, was as long as in fact it was, mainly from 1915-1965.

The word 'repertory' has been used in different ways, and as I believe meaning is mainly a matter of use, the meaning has varied. There is the use of the word to refer to those companies where a number of plays were produced, and these were played at different intervals and for varying lengths of time; but the term repertory is more usually employed to denote companies which play each production for a limited period, generally one, two, or three weeks.

During this period I have listed over 250 towns where Reps existed operating on the basis of a weekly change of play. Some lasted only a few months, a considerable number for more than a continuous run of over 20 years. The longest appears to have been the company at the Pier Theatre, Hastings, which lasted from 1933-1964.

It may help with the historical perspective to consider that when Plymouth Repertory company was finishing in 1935, after 20 years continuous existence, the York Citizens Theatre was being founded, which ran on a weekly basis, for almost thirty years.

Weekly Reps were, in the main, a provincial theatrical activity. Most of the productions in the West End of London were of plays which ran for a much longer period.

The Weekly Reps arose, or more generally, the Repertory movement arose, because of dissatisfaction with the theatrical fare that was then available.

It was, not only true of the numerous companies that ran on a weekly change basis but it was also true of the companies, such as Birmingham, Manchester, and Liverpool, who played often on a fortnightly basis, or in some cases, three weeks.

There is a tendency today, for those who believe that all weekly repertory was of rather a poor quality, to feel that all that is necessary is more time and more money and you are bound to get a better end product. I hope I shall show that by no means was this true. If time alone could guarantee a good end product then every amateur production done during the fifty years of the Weekly Reps' existence should have been better as they certainly had more preparation time; and it would be foolish to deny that some amateur companies achieved a high standard and some still do but, in the main, this was not the case.

The fact that many experienced actors (this denotes male and female) stayed in the Weekly Rep companies, for long periods, is stressed by Ronald Russell, who managed the Little Theatre, Bristol, on a weekly change basis for, 14 years, and Reggie Salberg, of the well known Birmingham theatrical family amongst others, as a contributory factor to the high standard of acting often achieved. Ronald Russell states "between 1915 and say 1950, you were not in the era of T.V. and so many good and highly experienced actors were free and willing to work in Weekly Rep (especially if they were bringing up a family and with the prospect of a long season or sometimes series of seasons). Ralph Hutton, for example, spent 11 years under the old B.L.T. management and then came back and worked for me from 1936 till his death in 1944 and I remember him as a very fine actor indeed". Reggie Salberg comments, "Weekly Rep was a far from desirable system, of course, but some remarkable work was done. Actors of maturity stayed longer as there wasn't the lure of T.V. then and it was possible to have an ensemble". This is something that is rarely experienced today in regional repertory.

Repertory theatres came into being mainly in one of three ways:

1. A private theatre owner engaged a repertory company. This was the case at the Birmingham Alexandra Theatre in 1927, when Leon Salberg founded a repertory company there, a well known Birmingham theatre which is still operating today.

2. A wealthy patron financed a repertory company, either renting a theatre, or, as in the case of Barry Jackson in Birmingham, building one.

3. A syndicate of local people, often comprised of businessmen and educational personnel, formed a company; they put up the initial finance either, to rent a building, and then, later, perhaps to build their own theatre.

The Repertory theatre movement as such came into being in 1908 when Miss Annie Horniman (who inherited a considerable fortune from the family association with the distribution of tea – a beverage that appears to have done more to succour the English in times of adversity than all of the theatres put together), bought the Gaiety theatre in Peter Street, Manchester, and established a company producing plays for a definite period of time, and which gave first showing to a number of plays by Northern playwrights. 'Hobson's Choice', which is still played today in existing reps, was one, this has been produced for television, and a film was made of it with Charles Laughton starring in the leading part.

The next major city to see the formation of a repertory movement was in Liverpool. A public company with 1,300 shareholders began its career at the Playhouse on 11th November 1911. It was difficult at first; unlike Manchester and Birmingham there was no generous wealthy patron. However, they persevered and the repertory attracted a regular audience.[1]

In the spring of 1913 in Birmingham, Barry Jackson presided over the opening of the first ever repertory theatre built in Britain.

Earlier I suggested that many young people today, and particularly young people who are involved in theatre activities, are bewildered in considering how the companies of that period managed to put a play on each week. Had it just been the one

3

play for one week, this conceivably would have been possible and understandable; but to put on a play, and during the first week's run of that play to rehearse and prepare another one, and to do this for up to 45 weeks of the year, with a break for Christmas – though usually this would not be the case; the break would be taken probably in the summer months for three or four weeks, the Christmas time being occupied with some kind of pantomime or review entertainment. This, of course, also being produced, prepared, and acted by the members of the repertory company!

So today with three, four, five, or even six weeks, as is the case at the Royal Exchange Theatre in Manchester, contemplating putting on six plays in that period of time, it is understandable that they should feel that the end result of what was presented must have been pretty poor. However, it is as mistaken to make generalisations about Weekly Rep, as it is to make generalisations about the present day state of regional theatre. There were so many Weekly Reps and one must, I think, face the fact that the history of regional repertory theatre is really, at least for 50 years, the history of the Weekly Reps.

In their book 'The Repertory Movement' Rowell & Jackson [1984] devote at least half of the book to repertory since 1960; this being the period, of course, when repertory theatres have been subsidised and a longer preparation time was, and is, possible.

Those who have made evaluative statements regarding the Weekly Reps have tended almost to dismiss it without any further consideration, certainly without any further research, which is rather surprising in view of the fact that there were so many towns where there were Weekly Rep companies. Rowell and Jackson [1984] write "we must now consider the phenomenon of Weekly Rep" – that is why I have subtitled my book 'A Theatrical Phenomenon'. The phenomenon is that, with so relatively little time, and with so many plays to produce, a good standard was attained in many of these theatres. It is so easy to fall into the trap of generalising from a particular instance. For example, Peter Nichols, in his autobiography 'Feeling Your Behind', records his experience of Weekly Rep, in the early 50's, at Yarmouth and Frinton-on-Sea.

He says "At Yarmouth, in winter, I played leads in the Aquarium, a Weekly Rep doing A. A. Milne and Ben Levy to houses of 30 pensioners. These were Weekly Reps, standards were low, houses were small." Without subsidy no theatre would have lasted very long with an attendance of thirty pensioners! This was Weekly Rep at Frinton-on-Sea in the early fifties. Had he, for example, been playing at York in the late 1930's, he would have been playing weekly to 10,000 people who came from all walks of life.

It must be very galling and frustrating for young people, who are not old enough to be able to remember any Weekly Rep performances, to hear people, who are old enough; and there are quite a lot of people around still, as my correspondence from all parts of the country has confirmed, recalling quite remarkable things being done.

I am sure that a company somewhere could be found to fit almost any description. Here are two extracts from reviews of Shakespearian productions.

1.   "At the............ there is an earnest ramshackle and poorly spoken production of Macbeth. The sparse audience were mostly school children; to inflict such ill thought out and deeply boring work on them is an atrocity."

2.   "The production of Romeo and Juliet, and we say it deliberately, was the best production of this play that we have ever set eyes on."

I have no doubt that there are persons who would have no difficulty in stating which of those two extracts referred to a Weekly Rep company, number one. In fact, it is from a review by John Peter in the Sunday Times, October, 1984, of the production of the subsidised London Young Vic company.

The other one was a review by Alan Dent, who was one of the leading drama critics in the forties, of a production by the Wilson Barrett company at the Lyceum Theatre, Edinburgh. This company operated on a weekly basis for nearly ten years. Unfair? Of course; but no more unfair than the wholesale condemnation of Weekly Rep, which is implicit in the remarks of some of the commentators on this activity. Thus, for example, the childish petulance of Clive Goodwin, the T.V. critic for Tribune in 1966, "One of the great benefits brought about by the advent of television was the killing of weekly repertory. With few exceptions this provisional chain of rickety sweat-shops laid the foundation for everything that is bad in the English Theatre. Very few of our best and greatest actors ever

5

ffered them. Almost all our bad ones did."

Surely a case of not only getting out of bed the wrong way, but also tripping over the cat and falling downstairs too!

Nearer to our own time, Robin Thornber, a Guardian drama critic, writing about an attempt to run a Weekly Rep company at Crewe in 1985 wrote "Weekly Rep – the very name has become a term of abuse to the present theatre generation."

Those who are responsible for the distribution of Arts Council funds, to the various theatres throughout the regions, speak quite often of establishing 'centres of excellence'; and sometimes one is reminded of the man, whom the philosopher Wittgenstein mentions, who went out in the morning and bought several copies of the same newspaper to reassure himself that what it said was true. One sometimes feels that they think if they keep repeating 'centres of excellence' they will somehow materialise out of the air.

It is a sober reflection that genius may not be accredited to the Oxbridge graduate with a double first, and yet be manifested in the work of a Bedford tinker, or an Irish labourer.

Many of our subsidised theatre companies, who have considerable lengths of time, and far more money with which to prepare their productions, do not receive universal acclaim for their efforts.

One of the most misleading but, nevertheless, most comforting 'frames of mind', we can fall into is that of the 'living on a tradition' syndrome. By this I mean that the achievement of any group of people, which is praised at a particular time, is carried into perpetuity maybe long after that group, or company, appearing under the same name, has ceased to maintain the standards that warranted the initial commendation. Equally so, if a company or institution gets a bad name, this again may continue long after improvements have been made to the standard of work of that company.

Theatrical companies, that had a long life, must have varied in the standard of work presented over the years. Artistic work, of a corporate nature, seems often to have centred around an outstanding personality, such as Lilian Bayliss at the Old Vic, Joan Littlewood with Theatre Workshop, and Wilson Barrett with his companies in Edinburgh and Glasgow. The latter being the grandson of the well known Victorian Actor/Manager.

I also found that some of the assumptions generally associated with evaluative and descriptive remarks about Weekly Rep were more conjectural than the result of close examination, or personal experience.

Thus, for example, Norman Marshall, whose criticisms are to be found in 'The Other Theatre' [1947] states that "the actor who stays in Weekly Reps comes to rely on tricks which will enable him to get through a part even when he scarcely knows it".

Maybe some did but there is authoritative evidence to show that many of the actors who stayed with Weekly Reps developed into, and remained, fine craftsmen. I took with me to the Royal Exchange, Manchester production of 'Death of a Salesman' in 1985, a 33 year old memory of a Weekly Rep production of this play at the Coliseum, Oldham.

Leaving aside the fact that at the Exchange I was sitting in one of the two galleries where the sight-lines are poor (one has to lean forward to see what is going on beneath one) it was a competent performance.

If my memory of the Oldham production was not eclipsed, it was mainly due to the superb craftsmanship of an actor named John Barrie in the part of Willy Loman. The years had not made him into a 'trickster'. One of the parts was played by a youthful Bernard Cribbins; the sets designed by Claude Watham, and the production by Guy Vaesen.

I'm sure that some of the people involved in Weekly Reps, at times, felt exhausted, but a considerable number of my correspondents say that these years were amongst the happiest of their careers. "My time in Rep was amongst the happiest in my life – most particularly in Wolverhampton. What I learned in Rep has been the most valuable of all; especially team work, a sense of humour, dedicated work, great discipline, and making one cope with almost any emergency," writes Peggy Mount.[2] One feels that today, many of the personnel involved in Regional Reps are equally exhausted by anxiety as to whether they will receive sufficient grant aid to cover their costs.

Knowing that their continued existence depended solely on the takings at the box office, the artists in Weekly Rep were motivated by economic necessity; but it does not, necessarily, follow that they were unhappy in their work; or that standards were poor.

One of the great unsung theatrical families of this century is the Salberg family, for long associated with the Alexandra Theatre, Birmingham, and the Grand Theatre, Wolverhampton. There is no more respected family in the history of the theatre. The father, Leon Salberg, bought the Alex' in 1911, and his son Derek continued to manage this theatre until his retirement on 31st July, 1977.

The Salbergs were, unashamedly, commercial – something they had in common with the great Quaker family of Cadbury, who have produced quality chocolates, in their Birmingham factories, for many years. The Salbergs presented quality entertainment – including the annual pantomime, which saw the appearance of many well known names in light entertainment – for many years.

I find the slightly 'holier than thou' stance of the supporters of the Birmingham Rep and of the Manchester Gaiety theatre, rather amusing in view of the fact that it was only due to the commercial enterprise of their forebears; one faction in tea and the other in 'dairy products' – that Annie Horniman and Barry Jackson inherited the money to support their respective projects in the first place! However – praise be – they did not have to spend it on the two theatre enterprises associated with their names.

It is worth recalling that between 1913 and 1930 Barry Jackson spent £100,000 of his own money to keep the Birmingham Rep open.

This, surely, is the answer to those who say that had the Weekly Reps put on 'good plays' more people would have gone to see them and they could have run for longer periods. The Birmingham Rep could not attract sufficient people to cover the costs though, outside of London, it had the biggest catchment area in Great Britain.

If the response, in terms of the numbers seeing a play, is the criterion of a 'good play' then this makes 'The Mousetrap' (now in its 38th year) the finest play ever!

One does not need to be very conversant with modern aesthetic and moral philosophy to appreciate the difficulty of applying the description 'good' to any object or activity. The reviews by drama critics of plays performed, can vary so much as to lead one to question whether the critics were actually watching the same performance! As to what makes a play a classic, I favour Arnold Bennett's conclusion that "a classic is not a classic because of the consent of the majority; but because of the passionate few who, in all ages, discern its worth."[3]

Today, one may question the relevance, to our situation, of plays written by ancient Greeks, and playwrights of the first Elizabethan period. But, as they are performed from time to time, one is lead to the conclusion it is because they are about human beings primarily and not about members of this or that particular 'class'.

It may have done young Hamlet good if he had been compelled to get on his bike and go and search for work in Elsinore, instead of his material and nutritional needs being supplied without any effort on his part, and leaving him free to stand, sit, or mope around contemplating his predicament. One feels, however, that the attraction of Shakespeare's Hamlet is that he embodies and expresses human fears and anxieties, not those of a particular class. Above a certain calorie intake level, and a measure of protection from the climatic conditions in terms of clothing and shelter; there is no guarantee of happiness or peace of mind.

Agreed, there may be some truth in the old music-hall quip that 'Money doesn't guarantee happiness – but it does give one a greater variety of miseries'; but there is ample evidence around one to show that 'the rich' are not always in a blissful state, any more than are the poor (not the poverty stricken) in a constant condition of misery.

My own belief is that Shakespeare still appeals because of his consummate articulation of human feelings, coupled with the expression of aspirations and hopes in the heightened language of his plays. This, like the language of the Authorised version of the Bible, was not the language one would have heard in the streets of Stratford-on-Avon, or those in the vicinity of the Globe Theatre in Shakespeare's London.

I have heard, as a justification of the linguistic obscenities heard on the stage today, that these are as people "talk in 'real life'".

I am not aware that in 'real life' when people are murdered, they later get up, take a bow, and then go off to perform their normal, everyday, functions!

I'm sure that the Artistic Director could solve all of the National Theatre's financial problems in one evening if he could persuade Ian McKellen to play Macbeth in accordance with this 'real life' criteria. He would have to hire the Wembley Stadium to accommodate the multitudes who would, I'm sure, flock to see this unique event.

(Moral problem for the Director – Ian McKellen offers to make this sacrifice – should he accept?). But this would almost certainly be a 'no win' situation. Apart from the difficulty of finding an actor willing to kill and then decapitate Ian McKellen; there would be many in the crowds still sceptical about its authenticity — "It's not real – they are only acting... I bet Paul Daniels had a hand in that".

If this seems excessively puritanical let me add that I do swear – occasionally. In the main I agree with the writer (probably G.B.S.?) who said that swearing was a sign of a poor vocabulary; but it can be very economical when one is angry! However, it becomes monotonous and boring if constantly used. Seventy years ago people flocked to see 'Pygmalion' to hear the one line 'Not bloody likely' spoken by Eliza Doolittle; but G.B.S. managed to write some excellent dialogue without recourse to swearing.

The criticism that the Weekly Reps only played comedies, that had been successful in the West End of London, is again an over simplification. "Nor is the charge levelled against Weekly Rep that they only did popular plays (melodrama and farces especially) true. Here in Bristol we brought Chekhov to the City for the first time, but also included Ibsen, a lot of Shaw, Galsworthy, Priestley, Coward, as well as your more popular pieces like 'Rookery Nook' or the works of Miss Agatha Christie. It was certainly our policy to endeavour to cater for all tastes even if it sometimes meant losing money (which we certainly did when we essayed Strindberg)!," writes Ronald Russell. [4]

For most of the fifty years of their existence the Weekly Reps were, as with all theatres, subject to the scrutiny of the official censor, which ended in 1968.

I'm sure that no-one who had experience of, or has endeavoured to ascertain some facts about Weekly Reps, would wish to deny that some of the plays performed were trite and superficial. The extraordinary thing is the ample evidence that many of the 'good ones' were well acted and, as we shall see in the case of Northampton Rep, and others, extremely well provided for in terms of the settings.

One feels that many of the young actors today, who may have spent three years in a drama school, or university drama department are rather like the prospective carpenter and joiner who has studied the drawings of Chippendale, Hepplewhite, and Sheraton; has been to museums, and stately homes, to see examples of their work, but has no, or little experience, of making furniture. He must, if he is to achieve a high standard, begin to handle wood, 'sniff' wood, observe its texture and graining.

Sooner, rather than later, he must apply measuring equipment, and then a saw, followed by the use of a mallet and chisel, and the other tools of his trade.

Anyone who has watched a skilled potter place a lump of clay on the potter's wheel, and then proceed to mould and shape from this a beautiful vessel and who has then placed his, or her lump of clay and attempted to do likewise, and perhaps needing to make twenty efforts before getting something that resembles a vase to stay intact, will know what I mean. This is true, of course, of the acquisition of any skill. It all looks so easy!

At another level we all know how easy it is to 'love humanity' – it's ones real, live, next door neighbour who presents the problem; especially, if his dog comes and piddles on ones prize chrysanthemums!

There is little dispute, even by such stern critics of Weekly Rep as Norman Marshall, that a year or two working in Weekly Reps was valuable; and there is ample testimony to this fact.

A few years after making his criticism of Weekly Reps, quoted earlier, Clive Goodwin was in a more conciliatory frame of mind when interviewing three actors, all of whom had experienced Weekly Rep, but were now well known, namely Harry Corbett of Steptoe & Son, John Neville, and Robert Stephens.

To Harry Corbett he put the question "You were in a fairly ordinary commercial weekly repertory company?" "Yes. Ordinary in the sense that it had the usual inevitable pattern of theatres, but they all had an individuality of their own, these little repertory companies. This one was started by a man desperately interested in theatre, a scene-painter called Jimmy Lovell, one of the most splendid men I ever met. He'd been in the business for years. It was started by him, financially undercapitalised, until 'the committee' was brought in and that is the fatal stage.[5]

But I was started off by this extraordinary man; otherwise I wouldn't have been in the position I am now. I was taken to him by a friend, and he said, "Righto, we're desperately short; get on there, play a detective inspector, a cockney." This was terrifying, my cockney was foul. I walked on to the stage and I couldn't move and talk at the same time. I had to cross first, then speak; it was disaster. I said, "That's it, I'm off, I don't want to do any more."

Then he saw me in the street: "You, I want you. Didn't you get my letters?" "No, I didn't get your letters." "I want you!" "What is it?" "For the front legs of the cow in the pantomime." Well, what had I got to lose? So I played the front legs of the cow in the pantomime.

Successfully?

Yes, because I had eyes that moved, and ears that went like that on strings. I really tore the kiddies' hearts, you know what I mean? Nicked the show in other words. Because I was playing an animal. Jimmy Lovell obviously saw in this, funnily enough, a characterisation. I sometimes say, even though it was bovine, it was one of my best, he handed me down a little note – while he was madly working the lights – would I like to start work with him at thirty bob a week in the repertory theatre. It's only because of splendid men like this, in the individual repertory theatres, that there was a source of intake for the profession which was varied; instead of everybody coming from a specific area or a specific class."

To John Neville, now directing in Canada, "When you left the Park your next job was a season of weekly repertory at Lowestoft. Now I think this was your first and only dose of weekly rep. Was it a good thing for you?"

"Yes, I think so. It was one of the happiest times I've ever had in the theatre, possibly because one knew so little about it. It was extremely good for me playing a great number of parts very rapidly, with only a week to work on them. It's a horrifying thing to do, but it's a very good lesson in discipline and getting down to the job. But it's obviously something that one shouldn't do for long, one can get into bad ways of acting by taking short cuts and so on: I did enjoy it very much. I had the additional pleasure of working with a young director who was just new to the theatre himself, Stephen Joseph; we worked together on a number of mad projects at Lowestoft and had great fun."

Robert Stephens recalled his days at Morecambe. "After drama school you then did five years in various reps up and down the country. This must have left its mark on you in some way or other. Do you think it's a good mark or a bad mark?"

I think it's a good mark in the way in which I was very fortunate in doing it; I didn't stay in any particular kind of repertory company too long. The first job I had in rep was in Morecambe, I was there for sixteen months doing a different play every week. The amazing thing about it was that I was constantly being miscast, always playing old men, or parts which were not right for me. But you have to do them, and you have to do them in a week. You have to go on to the stage on Monday night with something. And I think that's very good, after a drama-school training, to be plummeted into something like that, where you are absolutely forced every week to do something different, something new, for yourself. Then I went into two-weekly, three-weekly and finally monthly repertory in Manchester; I think by that time I had assimilated all I could get out of reps."

"The kind of rep that you were in, weekly rep, has largely disappeared now. Do you think that's a good or a bad thing?"

"I think it's a bad thing for young actors because it teaches you a sense of responsibility. If you play thirty leading parts in a year, it does give you a sense of walking on to the stage and taking command of that stage, because you've just got to do it. I think that's a hard thing to learn in any other way, it's something that grows within you by constantly having to do it. But if you come out of a drama school and are plummeted straight into the West End or into television, then that's something which is difficult to learn." [6]

But what was the subsequent development of the thousands of actors who worked in the Reps between 1915-1965?

My opening chapter is a consideration of this question, followed by descriptive accounts of a week in the life of – a manager, the players, the producers, and the scenic designers, of working on this weekly change basis.

We then look at some of the companies in the North, South, East, West, and Midlands. This, of necessity, is selective, and it may be argued that these were exceptional companies. Equally, one might argue that an account of football teams over a similar period would be selective. Manchester United, Liverpool, Arsenal, would tend to be to the fore – though these teams could be found in the lower divisions during their life.

However, I do not intend to draw up a divisional chart of Weekly Reps! There are too many people around still who worked in them and I might risk a libel action.

There is no doubt that there were avaricious individuals who used Rep, or thought they could use Rep, to make a fast buck for themselves; and who were mean and selfish in their exploitation of the fact that supply always exceeded demand. The development of the actors trade union, Equity, was the response to this, and the present situation, which seems to be centred around the conditions of entry to Equity, is one of lively debate. The problem, experienced by all employers, of coping with the threat of the withdrawal of their labour by their employees if wage demands are not met, is not unknown in the theatre. However, if costs are more than box office takings, plus Arts Council grant, and local authority aid, then there is a problem.

There are few regional Reps existing on box office takings only today. But the story of Weekly Reps is entirely of theatres being run on the box office receipts. It was not until the late 50's and early 60's, that a few were considered worthy of grant aid by the Arts Council. It may come as a surprise to some that a company refused grant aid! "If we take their money we shall probably have those buggers coming up here and telling us what to do!"

Subsidy has been with us now, for more than 40 years and if, as we are told by Sir Peter Hall, Melvyn Bragg, *et al*, the Arts should be subsidised because they are necessary for the well-being of the nation's soul; it is worth reflecting on the fact that during this time the crime figures have increased; we have had rioting in our inner cities; there is a drug problem of almost epidemic proportions; and George Steiner has reminded us that some of the top Nazis were fond of classical music. During Stalin's ruthless dictatorship (now condemned by Gorbachev) the Bolshoi ballet and the Moscow Art Theatre continued to perform.

Professor John Pick remarks "We have grown used to equating the financial support to 'the arts' by government as a good indication of that country's civilization. Yet in truth there is no relationship between what a government spends upon the arts and the quality of life or the artistic products of that country. Hitler's Third Reich, Mussolini's Italy, Stalin's U.S.S.R. all

14

spent proportionately more upon the arts than Britain, Canada, Australia or the U.S. now do, but we would surely not take that as conclusive evidence of their superiority". [7]

Another suggestion is that because as many people go to the theatre as go to football matches this is another reason for subsidising the theatre! Reverse this and say that because as many people go to watch football as attend theatres the football teams should receive the equivalent subsidy. Close all of Manchester's subsidised theatres and there would be some despondency and protest: close Manchester United and City football grounds and.... be prepared to take to the hills!

There was not any competition from T.V., or even cinema in the early days, and I have plenty of evidence to show that the visit to 'their Rep' was the highlight of the playgoers week.

A correspondent from Hastings wrote "We started going to the shows on Hastings Pier at the beginning of World War II, after a while the Pier was closed to the general public and the company moved across the road to the White Rock Pavillion; sometimes the air raid siren would sound during the performance, the audience sat tight and enjoyed the play, although when the anti-aircraft gun behind the Pavillion opened fire it was difficult to hear what the actors were saying!

After the war the company moved back to the Pier, their fans still following; on a very windy evening the sea would pound against the girders under the pier and we wondered if we would be carried out to sea but whatever the weather we still went along every week, it was the highlight of the week."

It was for this reason that the audiences were of a social mix – people from the varied occupations, skilled and unskilled, high and low incomes, went to the local Reps. There may have been an element of 'natural selection' as to where they sat – 'working class in the gallery – aristocracy in the stalls' would be an over simplification of the distribution of the audiences if only for the simple fact that not all of the Reps had galleries; and some of the pioneering ones were not in purpose built theatres, but in halls adapted for theatrical use.

We find the late, well known commentator on show jumping Dorian Williams – whose family moved to a village near Northampton in the 1920's, recalling that "We were a very close, very, 'family' family. Although we had many friends, both as a family and as individuals, we were always content and self-sufficient amongst ourselves, preferring to do things together, whether it was hunting, exercising the horses, going to shows or point-to-points; or to a theatre, only very rarely in London, but almost every week to the Northampton Rep." [8]

I hope, in what follows, that I shall show that this theatrical phenomenon was far more diverse and complex than is usually thought to have been the case – there was nothing like it before in theatre history; and for it to occur again television and subsidy would have to disappear – an unlikely event.

There were remarkable men and women working at this level – all of them 'human – all too human'. I have little for the prurient mind; not because there was no sexual misbehaviour, no jealousies, no hatreds, no pettinesses – but, because these are human weaknesses; not something peculiar to theatrical personnel. Equally there was dedication, discipline, generosity, respect, and humour.

---

[1] 'The Liverpool Repertory Theatre' by G. Wyndam-Golding [1935].

[2] Letter to Author.

[3] 'Literary Taste' by Arnold Bennett [1909].

[4] Letter to Author.

[5] This company was, in fact, founded by Jim Lovell and Arthur Spreckley.

[6] From 'Acting in the Sixties' [1971].

[7] From 'The Arts in a State' by John Pick. Published by The Bristol Classical Press [1988].

[8] 'Master of One' by Dorian Williams [1978].

Chapter 1

Time and Chance

"I returned, and saw under the sun, that the race is not to the swift, nor the battle to the strong, neither yet bread to the wise, nor yet riches to men of understanding, nor yet favour to men of skill; but time and chance happeneth to them all".

Ecclesiastes

One might add "Nor yet stardom to those with 'star' qualities". It is a fairly safe assumption that, if there are one hundred applicants for a job, at least ten of the ninety nine who failed to get it would have done the job just as well.

There is evidence to demonstrate this in the theatre of understudies taking over, owing to illness, or some other misfortune, befalling the leading player.

Peggy Mount, who spent some years in Weekly Rep and became well known for her performance in 'Sailor Beware' (this ran for a 1,000 performances in the West End) wrote, "Yes, it is quite true that someone else was offered the part of Emma Hornett originally and was unable to take it on, which was my good fortune!" [1]

In a profession, where supply so far exceeds demand, there are bound to be some disappointed actors around. This is, of course, true in other employment: bank clerks who never become bank managers; teachers who never become head teachers, and so on. People are 'pipped at the post' and must either learn to accept it and, in some cases, gracefully concede that the person chosen deserved it, waiting for another opportunity to arise; in the meantime doing their best.

It is not uncommon to meet references to the contention that the Repertory movement was a good training ground for the acting profession.

So we find Phyliss Hartnoll in 'The Oxford Companion to the Theatre' saying, "At its best the old repertory theatre was an excellent training ground for young actors. A weekly change of bill, with the strain of rehearsing one play while acting in another and learning lines for a third, and the added tension of frequent first nights, could do harm, and most actors remained in repertory only for a year or two. Yet it made for versatility and resourcefulness, was excellent for training the memory, and soon gave beginners self-confidence; many excellent players graduated from weekly rep."

These cautionary remarks are found again in 'Theatre of Two Decades' by Audrey Williamson [1950] who concedes that she had little personal knowledge but states, "The best repertory theatres, such as those at Birmingham, Liverpool, Oxford and Northampton, have displayed remarkable breadth of taste, ranging from Shakespeare and Shaw to O'Casey and Christopher Fry; and the experience they provide for the young actor is invaluable. An actor can stay in repertory too long: the weekly or even fortnightly grind inevitably produces a dependence on tricks, and few parts can be seriously studied or developed. But players without this variety of experience, in all types of characters, rarely reach the top."

John Haerem, MBE, who began his theatre career at the Manchester (Rusholme) Repertory company states, "Weekly Rep was a marvellous training ground. It demanded great discipline and team work. I learnt far more from it than the Drama school I attended, run by Michel St. Denis, George Devine and others who ran The Old Vic just after the second world war."

We think of training as a period when we attend a course, which may be for a few months, or for three years, as is the case in the Teachers' Training Colleges. It may be salutary to compare the conditions that have to be fulfilled in this area compared with the 'open to anyone' situation regarding entry to the theatrical profession.

That is 'open' in the sense that anyone can try to join a theatrical company to enable him, or her, to obtain an Equity card. The acting profession is a closed shop situation, and recently there has been a lot of discussion on membership of Equity.

Of course, there have been drama schools, or colleges, where one could train for the theatrical profession. The Royal Academy of Dramatic Art (RADA) being one of the well known ones, but attendance at one of these institutions was, and is, not a necessary condition of entry to work in the theatre. To be a teacher one must have successfully completed a course of training recognised by the Department of Education and Science; and, until recent years, those who did this were able to secure a post in teaching; and 'secure' meant that, short of committing some appalling act, one was in for life; and if one had to finish earlier than the usual retirement age, then good compensation terms were, and are, awarded.

In the theatre a job may only mean employment for the rehearsal and public presentation periods. The actors would then, like God on the seventh day, be 'resting'. Many, alas, would be 'resting' for long periods, but a small percentage, of all those who have entered the theatrical profession, would manage to find work on a regular basis, some becoming stars, the majority good practitioners of their craft. Two such being Ray Mort and Richard Vernon, both being members of Weekly Repertory companies in the fifties, of which I was the Scenic Artist, but whom one still sees, from time to time, on the television.

The assumption then that actors trained in the Repertory theatres (weekly, and others) and then went on to 'higher things' is mistaken. They either stayed in 'Reps' or gave up and sought other employment. It is difficult to ascertain the actual number, of the thousands employed in Repertories, who have become well known, but I am confident it would be no more than 5% of the total.

However, following the remarkable observation of the writer (2,300 years ago) quoted at the beginning of this chapter, I contend that there were many actors in Weekly Rep who remained skilled practitioners. The illogicality of the contention that if actors stayed for more than two years in Weekly Rep they would deteriorate needs to be stressed. From whom then, would these apprentices learn?

We have already met Ronald Russell's observation on Ralph Hutton, who worked for 19 years in this area (confirmed by Sir Michael Hordern... "I remember a senior member of the company – a fine actor – one Ralph Hutton"). Ronnie Barker writes of Glenn Melvyn, with whom he worked for two years in Weekly Rep, and of whom he says "A wonderful actor and very funny man, he was also a nice man – it doesn't always follow. He taught me virtually everything I know about comedy". He was in Weekly Rep for many years. [2]

I am grateful to Diane Glyn, who, with her husband, worked

in Weekly Repertories for 30 years, for showing me their 'date book' of all the theatres they played in. With as many as 250 companies operating throughout the country during the thirties, forties and fifties, it was not so difficult to find work if you were prepared to move around, and accept the weekly change situation. Understandably not everyone wanted to do this and, as the majority of regional repertories were weekly repertories, the alternative openings were few and far between.

The justly acclaimed achievement of Laurence Olivier, Ralph Richardson, and Peggy Ashcroft, help to give an aura of distinction to the Birmingham Repertory, where they were players in their early days, in much the same way as other institutions are given importance because of the subsequent fame of some of their students, or members of staff.

Harrow public school claims Winston Churchill, Pandit Nehru, Byron and others. It would seem to be a dubious distinction if only one or two, of the thousands of pupils attending a particular school, subsequently performed in some outstanding manner. Civilised society appears to be the product of unknowns who can be trusted to do a regular job of work. The signalman who can be trusted to set the points correctly on the railway line; the water works employee who helps to keep a supply of unpolluted water flowing to our houses, and similar public servants.

Today there is also the more awesome necessary requirement of a supply of highly trained scientists to maintain the nuclear powered industrial complexes. Unlike the steam and electrically powered establishments these cannot be 'switched off' and left; or closed down and then abandoned.

We are fortunate in having the names of the actors and actresses who played, at some time or other, up to 1963, at the Birmingham Repertory theatre.[3] I sent this list to people with an interest in the theatre asking them to state the names of those listed whom they thought had become well known, and they averaged 100 out of a total of just under 2,000 names, or 5%.

However, the Weekly Repertories tended to have their local 'stars'. As I have previously stated, actors tended to stay with the same company for much longer periods. Derek Salberg, writing of the Repertory company at The Grand Theatre, Wolverhampton says, "The company included an actor called

Gerald Cuff, to whom Kenneth More referred in his book as "one of the best actors with whom I ever worked and from whom I learnt so much". Kenny had joined the company a year or two later, and I recall that on his marriage to a member of the company I raised his weekly salary from £9 to £12!

During the years Wolverhampton nurtured many artists who were to become stars; notably, apart from Kenneth More, Barbara Mitchell, Peggy Mount, Rosamund John, Peter Vaughan, John Barron, Vanda Godsell, Nicholas Selby, Pauline Yates, Gwen Berryman (Doris Archer in 'The Archers') and Leonard Rossiter, to name but a few. *It included too, many fine actors, who never became stars, but were the backbone of companies like Wolverhampton, such as Aletha Orr, Lee Fox, Tommy Raynor and Penelope Shaw; a list which I could extend over several pages.*" [4]

John Barrie, another outstanding actor, was at Oldham and York Weekly Repertories for many years.

Undoubtedly, time and chance, played a big part in the destiny of the provincial actors.

One has to remember that the reputation of different companies varied, sometimes perhaps, unfairly; and it would be considered a 'step up' to move from one provincial repertory to another.

There is an understandable ambivalence with regard to the Repertory companies and those members of which became well known. On the one hand, there is pride in the knowledge that an actor, who had gained early, and subsequent experience, with a particular repertory company, had gone on to achieve national recognition; and on the other, the assertion that in the repertories there was no place for 'star' performers. The success was due to teamwork, and the willingness to undertake some of the necessary, though less congenial, tasks of working in 'Rep'.

If the assumption that all of the outstanding actors of a repertory company achieved national recognition was true, this, in view of the statistics previously mentioned, gives Birmingham Rep a poor reputation; only 100 out of 2,000! That this repertory company became one of the premiere 'Reps' was, surely, due to the many fine actors, and producers, who worked there as members of a team.

However, not even this company could please everyone.

Louise Macneice, who was a classics lecturer at Birmingham University during the thirties, in an article on the Birmingham Rep regretted that the theatre did not attract "the most intelligent people" in the city (that is staff and students at the University, where he taught), but drew its audience from various types of women seeking escape from their daily lives: Suburb dwellers, spinsters, school-teachers, women secretaries, proprietresses of tea shops, all these, whether bored with jobs or idleness, go to the theatre for their regular dream-hour off. The same instinct leads them which makes many hospital nurses spend all their savings on cosmetics, cigarettes and expensive underclothes. [5]

[1] Letter to the Author.
[2] From 'It's Hello From Him', published by New English Library [1988].
[3] 'The Birmingham Repertory Theatre' [1963] J. C. Trewin.
[4] 'My Love Affair with a Theatre' D. Salberg [1978].
[5] From 'Selected Literary Criticism of Louis Macneice' OUP [1987].

Chapter 2

A Week in the Life of............

"Depend upon it, Sir, when a man knows he is to be hanged in a fortnight, it concentrates his mind wonderfully".

Samuel Johnson

There is no doubt that the preparation of a play, followed by another play, and so on for as many as forty five continuous weeks in a year, called for an exceptional kind of effort and, indeed, a formidable concentration of the mind on the part of all concerned.

That some of those who started on this course gave up is not surprising. It involved almost Herculean feats of memorising and self-discipline to cope. One suspects that some of those who are most vociferous in their criticisms of Weekly Rep suffered the humiliating experience of not being able to memorise lines and, consequently, not being able to act their best, on top of coping with the common place chores of daily life.

In one respect it is mistaken to think of each production existing in isolation from the others. Though, not an exact parallel, because the theatre is a corporate activity and the painter/artist a solo performer but if, as an artist, I have to draw portraits of ten different people, but I am only allowed half an hour for each one, it would be mistaken to think that each effort existed in isolation from the rest. When I started the second one I should have acquired some technical know-how from my first effort. By the fifth one a swifter assurance in draughtsmanship and insight regarding the character of the sitter. The final one would be a consummation of the previous nine. Of course, given the whole five hours to the first one, no doubt, the end product would contain nuances of light and shade, of characterisation, that might well be missing from the others. On the other hand there are art enthusiasts who prefer Constable's sketches to his finished products!

So 'that was the week – that was' saw a similar routine being followed by most Weekly Rep companies from Plymouth to

Dundee. Of course, the routine differed depending on one's role in the company.

I was fortunate to contact Mr. Joseph Walker, who managed the Theatre Royal at Leicester, from 1950 to 1956, and in response to my suggestion that he write an account of a week in the life of a Weekly Rep manager, provided me with a description which is both informative, amusing, and forthright. It was a 'commercial' concern and the difficulties were compounded by 'the impresario' renting two other theatres, one of which was a variety theatre. The Theatre Royal did sufficient business to cover the expenses there, but some of the profits had to go towards making up the losses at the variety theatre, and it was this factor which led to the ultimate closure of the theatre.

The theatre was demolished soon after 1958 but, fortunately, we have a good record of its appearance, both exterior and interior. Richard and Helen Leacroft, the theatre historians, both worked there during the forties and there are illustrations of it in their books 'The Development of the English Playhouse' [1973] and 'Theatre & Playhouse' [1984].

The general picture is that of a person having to spend a lot of time in the theatre, for almost seven days a week, coping with the general matters of box office bookings, checking and re-stocking bar requirements, dealing with the non-acting members of staff such as cleaners and usherettes, along with the other demands from suppliers of goods necessary to maintain the theatre and the constant 'discipline of survival' needed to balance the books and provide money to meet the weekly staff and artists wages bill. In his own words "the latter brought on the usual teetering nervous breakdown (a weekly event) since they brought home to one the hopelessly narrow financial margin on which such an establishment was run."

(At the time of writing we may think that, with subsidies, this anxiety neurosis is no longer in evidence, but the daily reporting of financial difficulties with regard to this or that theatre, suggests that it is far from absent).

On the other hand, professional theatre personnel sometimes need to be reminded that this condition is not peculiar to theatre. With so many businesses going bankrupt each year the constant demand for increased subsidy, on the part of theatre personnel is, understandably resented by business people who have to try and cope or else close down.

Joseph Walker describes a typical Monday. "Soon after arrival at the theatre the collating of all monies taken for the three performances on the previous Saturday, i.e. all monies from performances, from bar, ice cream, and confectionery sales, the bank books made up and all readied for paying-in. It was always the duty of the manager to take cash to the bank. Before the trip could be made, however, orders left by the barmaids, there were three bars, had to be collected and the requirements phoned through to suppliers by the licensee (i.e. manager), the secretary would check ice cream and confectionery stocks and orders phoned to suppliers for these items and usually the 'electrics', 'cleaning departments' and 'scenic departments' might have their requirements which had to be seen to. The bank trip, after all these matters had been expedited, could then be undertaken. This last responsibility was quite pleasant, it was a relief to escape. After leaving, a return to the theatre to reassure oneself that all was peaceful, by which time a light lunch was signalled, then a return home for a break, with a fervent hope that there would be no telephone call from the theatre. A return to duty was usually planned for about 4.30 in the afternoon. Between 4.30 p.m. and 5.30 p.m. a discreet savouring (with no interference in any way) of how Monday dress rehearsal was proceeding and friendly chat with the producer to ascertain if any material difficulties had arisen. Then came the time to begin to think about changing into evening dress ready for the first house performance of the new week's play. 'Changing' was significant, it indicated a new role (a rather more pleasant one) a new approach, a meeting with friendly people and on a Monday, in one's special seat, to view the running of the play, its quality in content and standard of playing and production, assessment of audience approval (or disapproval), possibilities that it would be popular, discussed in the town, probabilities that it might evoke a ticket demand that would be sufficient to pay our way out for that week. All these observations, recordings and impressions as material for the, sometimes, lengthy report which would have to be compiled, by the manager of course, and sent to the head office on the following day."

Going through the mail of that day he discovers "a letter from head office to say that the chief and his wife will be passing through Leicester on Monday, the same day the letter is being read, they should be arriving at about 11 o'clock, they would like to discuss next month's programme. It all comes down to the fact that from the moment they arrive the rest of the day must be given to them. One must be unhurried, eternally diplomatic, polite, cool and patient. They will be blandly unaware of commitments, daily routine or programme. They expect undivided attention. Changing time only will be the release, when, realising their manager really is committed in this instance, only then will they depart. Still they will not have arrived yet. Get the banking money all set up, no chance of getting to the bank but it can be paid in tomorrow with the coming nights takings. The banking exercise is just about finished when there is a call from the box office (there are always calls from the box office). The chief fire officer is downstairs, can he come up and see the manager, he wishes to discuss a matter of some importance? Yes he can come up. He couldn't very well be stopped anyway, he is a man of some importance. The 'matter of some importance' is known to the manager. The safety curtain descent during one of the previous week's performances was too slow and inaccurate with the time laid down in public safety regulations. The chief fire officer is friendly but official and forthright. A second check will be made that week and if the descent is still inaccurate an official report (to be avoided at all costs) will be made; on such a basis a chief fire officer could close the theatre until matters are righted. This time one is fortunate, there will be one more check sometime during the current week (no evening stated) if still inaccurate a further 48 hours will be allowed to put it right, after this time limit a further check will be made and if still inaccurate, then real trouble. A worry this sort of thing, there is only one firm, in London, of course, who can deal with safety curtains. That means an engineer comes up from London, works on the curtain for the day, issues a certificate of worthiness (always accepted by the Fire Authority) stays the night in the town and returns to London the following day. All that means a fairly hefty bill, a blow for a little theatre run on a shoestring. The chief officer departs, the manager returns to his office and there waiting for him are the chief and his wife. All is amiability, no mention of safety curtains, programmes, bills or disagreements. They do not care to hear about such things, they are pleased that the theatre is running so smoothly. They settle down in the office chairs, tea and biscuits are sent up from the box office. They have all the time in the world, they settle in for a long cosy chat, and talk about plays and plans and profitability and occasionally there comes, echoingly through the auditorium into the office, sounds of hammering, shouts of "a bit higher", "a bit lower", "now try the lights on it", etc. Behind all the amiable exchanges in the office, work is going on, problems are being solved, the sweat of creation hums and buzzes and striving toward deadlines is in the air. Soon it is lunchtime, an invitation to lunch will be forthcoming. There is no invitation. The chief and his wife have decided to be upon their way, they have elsewhere to go. A great relief, down to the bank then and deposit the money. After this a break, back home for a couple of hours and get back to the theatre for about 4.00 p.m."

This theatre, like many of the Weekly Rep theatres, performed twice nightly and so about 5.30 p.m. it was time to change into evening dress. He continues, "the happier and more pleasant and more fulfilling aspect of a manager's life is about to begin. All the trials, placations, bills and constant devious action to overcome difficulties take their place as the underlying subscriptions toward the payment that must be made to make possible the realisation of all this activity into an enjoyable evening for many people, to hammer it all out into theatre. The automatic heating (in winter anyway) has switched itself on. Its quiet almost inaudible hum embarks a stirring of life within the place and the warmth that begins to seep through the building augers the onset of the comfort and entertainment that is about to come. To celebrate this nightly event a suitable mode of dress is required, i.e. evening dress, rather like a guards officer who dons his ornate uniform in order to ride forth and honour an occasion. After changing, the commissionaire, a very important figure who requires a natural geniality that endears him to patrons, will have arrived. The auditorium foyer and bar lights all come into play. The commissionaire, smart in his maroon uniform, will take his pressure spray into the theatre and send an even scented mist over each of the three levels of seating. The five cleaners, under a good head cleaner and who work at mornings only, will have done a good job and even the canvas nosecaps on the red stair carpets will have been blancoed (whitewashed), and it gives an impression of smartness. The usherettes, two in the stalls, two in the circle, one in the upper circle, will have arrived and changed into their smart black and white uniforms. They are middle-aged, reliable, respectable ladies who enjoy their little part-time job. Young, modern girls do not fit the bill, they are too unreliable and since the patrons themselves are of a respectable middle strata of society they much prefer the older ladies with whom many are on the friendliest of terms. The bar maids, again all older women and very experienced in bar work, have opened and set up their shining smart bars. The usherettes stand at their doors, the commissionaire at the front of the house. The manager goes to the front of the stalls, he calls to each section of the house, stalls, circle, upper circle and the senior usherette calls back that all is in order, which indicates that all lights function, but above all the secondary gas lighting is functioning. Visiting fire officers keep a sharp eye open for any which are not operating and it is easy for the commissionaire to miss lighting the occasional one when proceeding on his rounds just before opening. The manager, in somewhat splendid ceremonial fashion declares "The house is open". The commissionaire releases the safety bars on the main doors and the public begin to stream in. It is about 6.15 p.m. and the first house will commence at 6.30 p.m. There is a small box office on each floor level manned by part-time ladies who will have collected their appropriate unsold tickets from the main box office. Trade at these small box offices is often very good and useful for those patrons who have not booked beforehand. The night is cold but conscience tells the manager he must go to the main doors and stand by the commissionaire to greet the patrons as they come in. Evening dress is not very warm and even with a pullover under the white shirt the cold air on winter nights will begin to grip. Finally all are seated. The two pianists take their place at their pianos placed in front of stalls just below stage, they render their pre-prepared programme of short duration, they will have a longer session at the interval. They are heartily applauded, they are popular, they discreetly disappear through the small swing door just below stage. The house lights gently fade out, the doors on each level are closed, the heavy curtains drawn over them. There is a sudden quiet, expectancy in the air, the play is about to begin. The manager proceeds to the circle and takes, unobtrusively, his seat to see the play through and make his usual assessments."

When your continued existence is dependent, not only on the sale of tickets, but also on the sale of drinks and ice cream, his pleasure at seeing some of the husbands staying in the bars, during the last act, is understandable. He writes "The first interval of 15 minutes arrives, the house lights go up, the two pianists re-appear to give their interval programme. The manager looks in at the bars, they are very busy, a heartening sight; the cellarman who works in the mornings only, has re-stocked three bars as ordered by the barmaids, from the morning's delivery. From snatches of patron's conversation it is clear they are enjoying the production, a pointer to a good week. The bar bells warn, seats are re-occupied, the pianists take their applause and disappear into the bowels of the earth. The house lights go down, the second act is under way. It goes well, the play is what they like (entertaining). The players are on form and enjoying the good response they feel comes to them from the audience, the production has slickness and polish, one of those good Monday nights where all goes well. The short second interval of 5 minutes arrives. The bars still do some trade but most are eager to be back to see how it all works out. Invariably there are those few who do not go back, they stay at the bar and chat. That is not anything to do with the play; they bring their wives who enjoy the theatre, they do their duty by those wives by sitting through the first or first two acts with them after which they do what they most enjoy, i.e. staying at the bar and talking to others of the same breed. They are always most welcome to do so. Between them they will spend some few pounds. At last the curtain descends, the manager has been able to sit through the production, no contingencies have arisen and that is a blessing. The company receive enthusiastic applause, they have thoroughly enjoyed the play. The house lights go up, the doors are opened, the public begins to stream out. The manager races down to the stalls main street doors to say "Good Night". Many return the salutation with a smile and remark "Very Good", "Enjoyed it", etc., but their faces alone tell a manager all he needs to know. Apart from the prospect of good business, one thing gladdens his heart immeasurably, the play finishes on time, even better, a few minutes early. This is a vital consideration for a manager. Approximately a quarter of an hour is available between two performances. This allows a good, easy departure of first house audience and complete clearance of the theatre for the arrival of the second house audience. Patrons for the second house will be already queuing outside the theatre as the first house audience is streaming out. On a cold winter's night the public do not want to be standing outside, unprotected, for too long. Furthermore, and most importantly under the production line pressures of this weekly repertory, players, back stage staff and all concerned with the production will have a good fifteen minutes to unwind, have their cups of tea and their smokes in preparation for having to go through the whole exercise once again."

I have no doubt that the job of managing a theatre, where Weekly Rep was operating, was far more trying than that of any other participant in this demanding activity.

The producer would have considerable demands made on his tact and patience in his endeavour to extract the maximum effect in the minimum amount of time. The actors and actresses had to memorise lines, rehearse and play twice nightly. The scenic designer would find his imaginative faculty, and scene painting skills, exercised to the full. The stage manager and his assistants, would be engaged in a seemingly endless pursuit of suitable furnishings and 'props' ready for the following Monday. But their respective roles still had reasonably defined boundaries within which they attempted to fulfil their tasks.

The manager, of a commercial rep company not only had to keep an eye on a hundred and one different activities, but he was also subject himself to the scrutiny of the person – the Boss – who rented the theatre in the first place and engaged him to manage the theatre and to see that it made a profit.

As I have stressed elsewhere the context of 'commercial' in the sense of making a profit from the entertainment offered differed only in the respect of the profit going to the individual promoter. The company that was controlled by a syndicate used the profit made for the future promotion of the company and, when funds allowed, to improve the facilities of the theatre.

Those who saw in the theatre a means of making money, but who had little artistic perception – who were, in some cases, downright ignorant – could be persuaded by an ambitious producer to attempt a play that had only minority appeal, but which was presented to the 'Boss' as being a play that would attract people to the theatre who did not find the average weekly fare to their taste. That they might lose as many customers as would be gained was carefully omitted from the persuasive chat.

The fact of having to present the play twice every evening and, consequently, making the length of time required for its presentation a major consideration in the manager's assessment of its worth, is commented on by Joseph Walker with some bitterness, and, retrospectively, understandable resentment. He writes "On occasion a manager is confronted by the type of producer who considers a script sacrosanct. The suggestion that it can be reduced by anything up to 10 to 15 minutes could cause a Savonarolian eye rolling apoplexy as if a foul blasphemy had been uttered in the presence of that unbending cleric himself. More experienced, more mature, more adaptable producers will often be aware that any play can be judiciously cut without, in any way, damaging structure, and, in fact, very often tautening and compacting it in such manner as to markedly improving it. Running two performances in one evening demands the tightest of schedules. If a second house performance is billed to start at 8.30 p.m. and at that time the first house is still running, great inconvenience and complications can ensue. Most certainly the queue outside the theatre will have lengthened considerably. If it is a cold night many will be uncomfortable and in no good mood; not a good way in which to embark on an evening's entertainment. Many still sitting in on the first house who come from outlying districts will not all have come by car but by rather infrequent bus routes and these patrons will begin to be worried about missing their connection and, indeed, many will leave before the end of the play rather than suffer a long wait in the city until the next bus is available. Generally when the curtain finally falls there will be an increase in the tempo of normal departure and entry by the second house patrons which is not only uncomfortable but has about it an element of danger. There is little time left for those patrons who enjoy a leisurely drink at the bar before 'curtain up' to indulge themselves, with consequent loss of a considerable amount of bar business. Since running late in first house means that second house patrons must be got into the theatre as quickly as possible in order that the play can start without delay to try and recoup some lost time, players, back stage staff, and all concerned are robbed of that precious interlude in which they unwind and also recharge for the second run ahead. Of course the time lost is never recovered. Toward the end of the second house many, who really must catch bus connections have to leave before the play is finished; front of house staff, usherettes, barmaids, commissionaire are restless and itching to get away. The consequences of an indifference to this absolutely vital adherence to time brings the greatest possible discomfort in its wake, loss of revenue, some element of danger, and most certainly a disgruntlement among patrons that does not contribute to the future prosperity of the theatre. These occasions occur more frequently when a manager is confronted by the type of producer who is concerned to mount 'prestige' plays, in most cases to satisfy his own vanity, especially the type who used repertory as a stepping stone to the bigger things which they envisage for themselves, or they can easily be persuaded by equally ambitious members of the company who press for inclusion in the programme the sort of plays in which they, those particular members, find parts in which they feel they would be splendid. It proved to be a constant law that plays selected on the basis of egotistical urge alone were an invariable disaster. Many such plays were, at the time being dealt with, of 'the kitchen sink' variety, sponsored and foisted on the public by 'The Realists'. The public hated them. They were humourless, crude to the point of offensiveness, without story or form or a feel for theatre. Some plays were of the abstract school purporting to make subtle observations on the business of life, the comments made usually by people sitting in dustbins or coffins or speaking with heads emerging from a pile of sand. Some plays, of course, were at the other end of the scale. Sublime masterpieces by Shakespeare, great historical romances and turn of the century plays by Pinero, Shaw and Galsworthy. This last category, some of which were produced, proved most successful but they were too long, too complex in scenic change and structure, far too expensive in costumes, wigs etc., and general production and rehearsal for twice nightly repertory run on shoestring lines and operating within such a pressing time limit that allowed for only but the most straightforward and simplest of productions. A provincial city public did not wish to be instructed through the theatre, they did not want subtle interpretations from supposedly clever playwrights, life for them was basic, holding a job, running a small business, surviving. They looked to the theatre for some escape from such routine. They found it at the theatre when it gave them good comedy (which they loved) in farce (when it was well written and played) in good drama, certainly in good mystery plays (Agatha Christie) in all romances (sweet and sad) in the occasional dashing historical story. Their tastes were straight forward and perhaps simple. But what they wanted filled the theatre and what they wanted, generally, could be produced well and expeditely, and inexpensively, and well within the confines of theatre run on everyday factory lines to make money (for that was all twice nightly theatre amounted to for those who operated from a remote head office). Much against a manager's better and more experienced judgement and indeed protest, these esoteric choices were inveigled into the programme. The producer concerned would probably have captured the ear of the controlling power at head office and wooed him into believing that this particular play, if included, would greatly enhance the prestige of the theatre and show the local public what could be done. The power that could say "yea" or "nay" (rather gullible) would be won over. The producer's choice would be included in the programme. That was an order. Invariably these choices were, as has been stated, sacrosanct. No modifications, no cuts, out of the question. A manager could point out step-by-step all the inconveniences caused by, long-running, but to no avail, what was said fell upon deaf ears; he was confronted by concrete egos, encased in iron wills, augmented by minimal intelligence."

On Tuesday morning there would be a production conference when the producer and scenic designer would discuss with the manager any additional requirements such as furniture, costume and special effects for the forthcoming production. If it was a period play details would have to be phoned through to the supplier, usually in London. A list of the furniture would be presented to him and he would visit the local supplier to choose this himself – the stage director might be over generous in his choice!

The finalising of the layout for the printers had to be completed and this done he must now turn his attention to a phone call taken by the box office. He continues, "A call has been taken by the box office from the wines and spirits suppliers manager. Could the manager kindly drop in to see him if not too busy?, he would like to discuss a matter of some importance. The manager decides he would like to 'drop in' and see him. The wines and spirits manager is a kindly, friendly man who always keeps a rare, good sherry in the wines cabinet in his office and a couple of glasses are always forthcoming to a good customer. The theatre manager is well aware of the nature of 'the matter of some importance'. So three calls must now be made, the printers, the furniture, and wines suppliers. Fortunately all the key points are within reasonable walking distance of the theatre and not too much time is wasted in reaching them. To the printers first, all is settled there, the sheets will be printed that day and sent to the bill posters, the two lots of box office cards will be delivered to the theatre later in the day thus enabling them to be addressed and posted to individuals without delay. There follows the journey to the furniture suppliers. The proprietor with whom the manager deals is engagingly persuasive of so many things to have which would embellish so well the set requirements under discussion. Every item hired is charged separately which explains the dealer's enthusiasm that so much should be used. The stage director would be easy meat for this astute chap. He is expensive, added to which he likes to have a free advertisement in the programme pointing out that all the beautiful set furnishings are from his shop. On return of the furniture at the end of the run of the play his observant eyes examine every piece for any signs of damage. He secretly hopes there is some so that he can make a full selling price charge to the theatre. Damage indeed can easily happen especially in scene changes which must be executed within a very limited time and furniture and furnishings are often literally thrown from the stage to make way for the new settings. The requirements are finally settled, the manager will arrange with the carriers to call and collect on the following Monday morning at 9.00 a.m. The call on the wine and spirit suppliers is next on the list. The manager is affability itself, the glass of rare sherry is forthcoming and comfortably seated the customer confronts Mr. G across his handsome desk. The theatre manager listens whilst the 'important matter' is quietly detailed. It is exactly as expected. The outstanding balance of monies owing for goods supplied has now reached a figure which has made his main office accounts department anxious. He, the suppliers manager, is now under pressure. Can something be done, otherwise next Monday's delivery, when ordered, may not be forthcoming. A part payment of at least £200 off the balance would ease matters. He further explains, in the most friendly way, that the time is approaching when payment will have to be made in advance for each separate weekly order given. The theatre manager had long expected this condition would be laid down. Still, that had not quite happened yet. Parting is friendly and amicable. The theatre manager will call on Friday morning and pay off £200. On his way back to the theatre the manager is juggling in his mind how the promise can be kept. He has coped with so many such situations in the past that he has become expert, if not extraordinary devious, machiavellian, and contortional in these matters. The previous nights theatre and sales takings have not yet been banked. In the past year financial pressures have often become acute and he (the manager) tends now not to bank too quickly. He will hold the takings for the moment, pay the promised amount to the wines manager, obtain a receipt from him which will go with the weekly balance sheet to head office to cover the payment. Head office are fully aware of the difficulties and have now allowed their manager to cope with such matters in his own way. It seems, at times, as if they would rather not look squarely at the situation, their eyes are turned away and an underpaid, now dexterous manager will see it through for them. But dexterity developed through hard experience must finally be pushed to its limits by the overwhelming reality of facts. For the moment, anyway, survival is buoyant".

His account stresses the contingent nature of his occupation. Everything is geared to making enough money to cover the expenses and, hopefully, for a little more to send to head office to gladden the heart of the 'Boss', and to reassure himself that survival is likely for a few more weeks at least. This is important for all of the people employed at the theatre as some of them, including the manager, have wives and children to provide for.

All managers, whatever the business, have to cope with unforeseen matters arising during the week and in the theatre at this time they may have included the following items mentioned by Joseph Walker. The safety curtain may not be working properly and the fire officer, who may call at the theatre any time, will ask for this to be checked. In this particular case it was a specialist job and the engineer had to come from London – more expense. Diplomacy of a high order was called for when a misunderstood stage manager is complained about by the stage carpenter who is threatening to leave at once if the matter complained about is not attended to promptly. This in spite of the fact that news has just been 'phoned through, from the producer, to the effect that the leading lady is not at all well and may not be fit for the evening performance. No understudies in Weekly Rep so she must be medicated and a mattress, with blankets, provided at the side of the stage for her to rest on during the periods off stage. Not a frequent occurrence fortunately. If the illness was incapacitating then an urgent call had to be made to a London agent in the hope that a replacement, who knew the part, could be found.

Though the life was demanding it would appear there was one respect, rightly or wrongly, in which his life was not as difficult as it is for a manager today. There was not the rigid compartmentalisation – what someone has called the 'oval and round headed nail' union demarcation – God help a round headed nail man if he is seen knocking in an oval headed nail...... "All hammers down – OUT!"

Joseph Walker died on 31st December, 1986 and this makes his recollection the more valuable as the number of people who were actively involved in provincial Rep, between 1915-65, diminishes. I'm sure that other manager's recollections would differ on some points; and I do not necessarily agree with all of his views on the playwrights who emerged during the fifties; but his account of audience reactions to some of these are of interest.

❏ The Players

What of the principal performers – the players?

The most frequent comment about weekly repertory in this respect is "But how did they manage to memorise their lines each week? Surely there was a lot of ad-libbing?" On the face of it this would seem to be a fair comment, but all of my correspondents are agreed that words were memorised according to the script. This, of course, does not mean that there were not occasional lapses of memory – it would be extraordinary had there not been, I'm sure they still occur today.

The constant exercise of this faculty sharpened the wits and enabled the actors to speed up the time required for memorising their lines.

So, to the suggestion that there was a lot of 'ad libbing', there was an emphatic denial.

Janet Burnell, who was employed as a Leading Lady at Coventry 1935-36, and who was released from her contract on 11th May 1936 to play the lead in a West End production states "Absolute nonsense. Prompts were very rarely needed. The occasional slip-ups were invariably coped with by the cast itself, leaving the audience unaware of any mishap or lapse of memory. To learn quickly and accurately soon became a habit. Different people had different pet methods, many writing out their cues and parts for final assurance. The one common denominator being to *forget quickly* ... to wipe one's memory clear of the current play immediately after the last show on Saturday night.

I was told by an elderly actor that at the turn of the century doing two and sometimes three plays a week they would be told the gist of the play and then go ahead as best they could but that has no place in the Repertory Theatres you are considering."

Diane Glyn, who, with her husband, worked in weekly Repertories for thirty years states, "Rubbish – no-one ever ad–libbed in weekly Repertory. You *worked.* You were told when engaged that you were expected to be D.L.P. Do you know what that means? "Dead Letter Perfect" and we *were* – otherwise "OUT". What is more – we played in large two-tier, sometimes three-tier) theatres and we could be *heard.*"

Colin Bean, who worked with a few Weekly Repertory companies in his early days, and whom one can see with Arthur Lowe and John Le Mesurier in the 'Dad's Army' photo (Illustration 2.1) writes "When one Artiste asked "Where's the Prompter?" the Director said "Mr. Hanson pays you to learn your lines, he doesn't pay someone to do them for you. If you get yourself into a mess, you get yourself out of it" (the same still applies today in Theatre-in-the-round). Firstly, in twice-nightly, the plays were often cut to fit the performance times. Secondly, by the end of Monday night, having then done the play three times in one day, one, hopefully, had some idea of what it was all about! Yes, I can remember some brilliant ad-libbing over 'dries' people being 'off' and props going wrong. One really had time only to 'learn the words' and hope to God one knew them."

Lala Lloyd, who started at Northampton, where Errol Flynn was then a young actor, is equally as emphatic, "Certainly we memorised our lines! We had to be D.L.P. (dead letter perfect). Ad-libbing only took place if some unfortunate 'dried', when we always helped each other out. If you couldn't memorise lines, there was no place for you in rep. You say our wits were sharpened, you're right – our brains became, and have stayed, flexible – I and my contemporaries have stayed that way."

Geoffrey Wood, whose theatrical career spanned sixty years, made the following discerning observations on this matter. "All members of the companies I was in, or had anything to do with, all learnt the show – some scenes or lines I can remember clearly to this day. By doing this week in, week out, the brain was constantly used. Some people were rather slow studiers – they were still a bit rocky on certain scenes on Saturday but they had Sunday to revise and they did – we would have given any one not knowing their lines very short shrift – they would have just been sacked. The two authors I found very difficult to study were Shaw – because you could not transpose any of his lines. His command of English was such that you could ruin a scene by upsetting his balance of words. The other was Pinero – because of his phrasing, which again, had to be completely correct. Shakespeare was easy to study, it was just the length that I sometimes found horrific. In Ireland we were doing "The Merchant of Venice" and "Twelfth Night" I think in repertory on tour – Monday/Tuesday/Wednesday, – Merchant – Thursday/Friday/Saturday – Twelfth Night. I, as a young man, opened both plays and one night started Twelfth Night instead of The Merchant – to be made aware of my mistake by the character actor slowly turning his back on the audience, slowly shaking his head at me whilst opening his eyes very wide. My first speech that night was rather long."

Ray Cooney, the author of the successful farce 'Run for your Wife', and other plays,started his theatrical career in 1952 with a touring fit-up company in Wales, performing in village halls. He states "The company stayed four or five weeks in most venues performing from our own repertoire of approximately forty plays. The company performed six plays a week! When I first joined the Midland Productions I was broken in gently. I had to learn one leading and two supporting roles in the first week, and over a period of about twelve weeks I learnt the whole basic repertoire. You had to be DLP (dead letter perfect) or you didn't know which play you were doing. My learning ability improved at a tremedous rate and after a few weeks I was learning enormous leading roles in a couple of days".

In 1954 he joined one of Frank Fortescue's Weekly Rep companies at Blackburn. After his fit-up experience, and the discipline of memorising lines, he comments "For me Weekly Rep was 'a piece of cake' as far as the learning of lines was concerned. While the other actors and actresses would sit up until the early hours of the morning learning their lines I, because of my fit-up experience, could get even leading roles under my belt in a couple of days."

My own recollection, as a member of the company who did not have to memorise lines, is of the actors knowing their lines and only rarely having to be prompted.

The extraordinary thing about this was that not only did one have to retain the lines for this weeks play, but one had to

Illustration 2.1 Three who worked in Weekly Rep – John Le Mesurier, Colin Bean and Arthur Lowe

memorise those for next week. Fortunately, the parts varied in length, and a good producer would try to balance the load. If an actor had a large role to learn one week, he would have less the following. As early as 1928 Alfred Wareing was considering the organisation at Manchester Repertory (Rusholme) theatre. He comments, "One difficult Repertory Theatre problem has been ingeniously yet simply solved by Percy Foster. Most of us know that the production of a new play each week for long periods means a greater strain than any company organised on the commonly accepted lines, could possibly bear. He has therefore got together such a company that each member of it is capable of playing a leading part, and so by arranging the programmes in thoughtful order, the varying changes of casting give each player a reasonable pause before their next big part comes up to be tackled. The advantage of a company so organised is that every part is notably well played, for the lead of one week may be playing a 'three-page part' in the next production."

When Reginald Salberg took over the management of the Salisbury Repertory theatre in 1955, which was then operating on a weekly change basis, he began, for example, to experiment with alternative large and small cast plays and found that in this way at least a quarter of all the forty or so plays in the season could be given two weeks' rehearsal.

Correspondents, who were playgoers, sometimes actually observed a member of a company in the process of 'memorising'. Thus Mary Inglis, of Edinburgh, remembers a member of the Wilson Barrett company – "Stephen Ewart used to walk along Sandwick Place learning his words – looking at the book then folding his arms – quite unconcerned and probably never seeing a soul passing him."

Laurie Upton, who worked as an electrician and Scenic Artist at the Theatre Royal, Portsmouth from 1930 onwards remembers, "I have known of important cue lines written on the 'upstage' side of a fireplace, or pinned to the back of a settee, and 'ad-libbing' in the event of an unforeseen accident, but generally, the actors were almost word perfect, a condition which was established through years of experience. I have known them pace up and down in a property room, clutching their script and rattling through their lines, totally oblivious to all and sundry around them, all to have it right by Monday first house."

When an actor appears on a stage how much he or she needs in terms of technical assistance is a moot point. Historically, of course, there was no assistance. The actors in the Greek theatre managed to make themselves heard; the players at the Globe, and other Elizabethan theatres, spoke the words of Shakespeare, *et al*, with clarity and were understood.

The subsequent enclosed theatres were all without additional technical amplification and this remained true until recent times.

There is no doubt that clarity of speech, along with the ability to project their voices, without seeming to shout, was mastered by all the actors involved in theatrical presentation of plays from the earliest times to the present day. Certainly Irving and Tree, Bernhardt and Campbell, Olivier, Geilgud, Richardson, Ashcroft, Thorndyke, and the thousands of repertory actors and actresses who did not become 'stars', were heard by the members of the audience. The latter would have responded to inaudibility either by staying away, or, complaining to the management, or, on occasions, directly to the players!

The voice may sometimes fail but this is, and was, a rare occurrence.

❑ Producers

The task of producing a play each week was very demanding; and again it needs to be stressed that over the fifty year period the number of producers must run into the hundreds. Some of these would be actor/producers, but quite a number were employed solely to produce. Today it is more usual to use the term director, but for the period I am concerned with, producer was the most common term used.

He, or she, had to help with the selection of the plays (this would mean, on average, more than forty each year). They must vary the selection – too many on the same theme and the audiences would have been bored. Those who criticise Weekly Repertory on the grounds that they did mainly West End comedies and farces, seem to ignore the fact that these can vary enormously in their content and style and, consequently, some evaluative work is necessary.

On 20 March 1985 Robert Young died, aged 93. He succeeded

Herbert Prentice at Northampton in July 1932. Aubrey Dyas's account of him gives a fair picture of his background. "Robert Young's life had been crammed with adventure. Born in Manchester, he was faced with stern parental opposition when he first expressed a desire to go on the stage, and, in consequence, he did not visit a theatre until he was nineteen years of age and living in Buenos Aires. Shortly after, he worked his passage as a muleteer in New Zealand, where he first acted. On the outbreak of war in 1914, he enlisted in the New Zealand Expeditionary Force, being one of ten white men attached to a Maori regiment, and serving in Gallipoli, where he sustained severe shellshock, and in France, where he was wounded. After the war, he studied for the stage and had extensive and varied experience acting with Sir Frank Benson's Company, with the Stratford-on-Avon Festival Company, and in the West End; stage-managing for Arthur Bourchier for three years, and producing for Lena Ashwell at the Century Theatre. Thus, Mr. Young came well equipped to carry on the worthy tradition established by Mr. Prentice. Furthermore, for several years previously, Mr. Young had been a Member of Parliament for North Islington, and, therefore, Northampton achieved another claim to fame as the first Repertory Theatre with a former M.P. as its producer." [1]

In an article he wrote for a theatrical magazine, Robert Young states clearly the pressures the Weekly Repertory producer was subject to – he writes "It is the absence of time which proves the greatest stumbling-block to the repertory producer. Organisation is the essential condition of success, for no time must be wasted. I prepare each play in detail before starting my first rehearsal. Every move is carefully marked in my producer's copy, and all grouping arranged. *Of course, during rehearsals it is sometimes wise to make minor alterations, for one must remember that the artistes bring their contribution to the pooled work, and if an artiste is experienced and has technique, he can be of much assistance by the quality of his interpretation of a given part.* But actually rehearsing the plays is only one part of a producer's duties. There are about forty-eight plays to be chosen every year, and, of course, there are not enough really suitable good plays to fill in each week. For instance, we cannot produce every London success here. Some contain too many characters, others have a theme which may not appeal to local audiences. From London successes, one turns to the classics, and here again many problems arise.... This work of selecting plays is full of pitfalls. Not only must the plays be as good as possible: they must also be varied in their sequence, otherwise our audiences weary of similar themes. So that the plays have to be balanced one against another in plot, simplicity of setting, and size and nature of parts."

However, in spite of these restrictions, there was no sitting around bemoaning the lack of time and money, and trying to convince himself how much more wonderful the productions would be if these were available.

Knowing that the continued existence of the Repertory company depended on attracting sufficient people to cover the costs, the producer maintained a delicate balance between the exacting demands that weekly change made on all concerned, and the entertainment value of the performance he managed to coax from them in the course of a week.

Of his experience at Northampton he said "During my three years at Northampton, I have produced about 144 plays: we have never had a serious hitch. This is a tribute to the whole company and staff, who work together with fine co-operation and speed. I regard the mere feat of learning a new play weekly as a miracle of memory on the part of the artistes."

Ray Cooney's remarks on Directors are of special interest in view of his success in creating, what is a complex form of dramatic expression, namely farce. He writes of his first Weekly Rep experience after fit-up – "However for the first time I had a Director to contend with. Although the wise Director in Weekly Rep stuck very much to the 'moves' and stage directions described inFrench's acting editions of the plays, he had the opportunity to work on 'characterisation', 'motivation', 'relationships', the shape of scenes, the dramatic 'line', etc. etc. etc. So for me, for the first time, I began to understand the craft of the Dramatist and the 'art' of both the Director and the Actor in the theatre."

With well over 250 Repertory companies operating on a weekly change basis the quality of the productions must have varied enormously; but the holding together of a group of players and stage staff, called for considerable patience, firmness, and imaginative ingenuity; and, no doubt, as with today, some underrated the difficulties. There is today, in some quarters, a move to limit the power of the director and for the actors to have more say in the general development of the presentation of the play. Simon Callow has been the most vociferous in this outlook, and the players of the RSC have demonstrated a desire to be more involved. But, in the main, directors are much in demand, and the Manchester Royal Exchange, with a million pounds a year subsidy, has four Artistic Directors on its payroll for an average of nine productions each year.

❏ Scenic Designers

Lee Simonson remarks in 'The Art of Scenic Design' "an ounce of imagination is worth a ton of scenery". That limited finance did not prevent Mozart, Dostoevsky, Van Gogh, Beethoven and others, from creating outstanding works of art is self evident. That there have been wealthy people who have failed to create any works of art worthy of note, is not so self evident, but implicit in the small amount of artistic work created in relation to the considerable number of people who could afford to create, but who were not, and are not, dependent on the sale of their creations to support themselves.

The facilities for the creation of settings that existed in the provincial theatres, during the period we are considering varied enormously. Often there was little attempt made to create the illusion of the particular location that was the geographical and architectural background of the dramatic presentation.

For much of the twenty years of the Plymouth Repertory the same backcloth of an oak panelled interior was used. Of course, it may be argued that the important thing was the characteri-sation and the dialogue – the play, was the first priority – people knew it was a theatre – a place of make believe – and if one was held by this – then fine!

And this is basic to the theatre that is involved with the presentation of plays.

The visual aspect of seeing a play performed raises the question of how much is necessary in terms of the stage setting.

We know that a play, written for the theatre will often come over very well when heard on the radio. The setting is conveyed by means of descriptive dialogue and sound effects; the Eliza-bethan theatre was simple in terms of its staging, again relying on the stimulation of the imagination through evocative language.

At the beginning of the 17th Century, when the theatre was completely enclosed, the influence of the scenic developments in Italy began to make themselves apparent through the work of the architect Inigo Jones. This saw the beginning of what has become known as 'The Great Scenic Controversy'.

In his book 'Changeable Scenery' (Faber 1952) Richard Southern describes the beginning of this controversy which is still evident today. He states, "To understand the controversy we have to go back to that extraordinary, fecund, generative period where so many of the characteristics of our present theatre sprang, that of the masque at the Stuart court.

There, under James I, the first wedding of spectacle to stage took place. Spectacle there had been before in Elizabeth's day and in Henry VIII's; and – completely separately – the dramatic stage had been before, not merely 'been', but, in that being, had reached an apogee of its long existence. But James's court was to see the richest parts of each fused, under the lambence of the Renaissance mind, in one feast of brilliance that could boast the simultaneous radiance of such first luminaries as Ben Jonson and Inigo Jones, master-poet with master-architect.

The married name of the united arts was The Masque. Then hard upon this too-brilliant wedding followed the divorce, upon grounds of incompatibility of temperament.

Jonson turned on Jones and all his ways, and the purlieus of the court were dinned with as fierce a stream of invective as ever passed a master-word-stringer's lips. The union was dissolved, and behind it there was left among the offspring a flourishing babe with vitality so rude and lusty, and nature so unbiddable, that it is vociferous in our own day almost as it was in theirs."

Certainly today there is little evidence of the use of elaborate set designs, and the accompanying increased costs of their construction, being on the wane. One production in the West End – 'Bounty' – was slated by the majority of the critics, except for the ingenuity of the settings by William Dudley. These involved movement of a kind that called for engineering skills of more than an elementary nature.

Comparing provincial theatre programmes of the thirties, forties and fifties with regional repertory theatre programmes today, what stands out is the greater number of people em-

45

ployed on the administrative and technical side.

Jonson expressed his dislike of Jones's elaborate creations in a voice of a distinctly barbed and vituperative kind. He wrote:

> And I have mett with those,
> That doe cry up the Machine! and the showes!
> O showes! showes! mighty showes!
> The eloquence of Masques! what need of prose,
> Or verse or sense, t' express immortall you?
> You are the spectacles of state! Tis true
> Court Hiero-gly-phicks! and all Arts afford,
> In the mere perspective of an inch bord!
> You aske no more then certaine politique eyes!
> Eyes, that can peirce into the mysteries
> Of many colours! read them! and reveale
> Mythologie, there, painted on slit-deale!
> O to make bords to speake! there is a taske!
> Painting, and Carpentry, are the soule of Masque!
> Pack with your pedling Poetry, to the Stage,
> This is the Money-gett, Mechanick age!"

We shall see that in the case of Northampton Repertory theatre, the settings and costumes for the plays could be of a high standard, and there were other scenic designers who produced effective settings with very slender resources.

There was no place for the designer who was not also a skilled scenic painter and, hopefully, had some manipulative skills with woodwork, canvas, hessian, and techniques of property making, plus some knowledge of costumes.

Sets were made from a stock of flats, rostrums, steps and backcloths. There was usually a good supply of flats – sufficient to cover the week's standing set and enough to meet the requirements of the following week. Most of the Repertories employed a full-time stage carpenter, who would re-shape existing structures, and be responsible for striking the set (the only 'strike', surely where everyone works!) and erecting the new one.

This operation usually took place after the final performance on Saturday evening, though change-over arrangements varied from theatre to theatre.

The limitations of time and materials may have caused dismay to some of the scenic designers; but for others they were a stimulus to the imagination and one soon learnt a lot about colour and painting techniques.

Simonson stresses that a stage setting is only a setting when it is erected, lit, and the actors move within it (not against it as a mere background).

It follows that the realisation of ones designs is a rare thing nowadays, with production costs so high. The Weekly Repertory, and the fortnightly ones, offered the designer an opportunity to see his 'ideas' realised, and he did not have to wait long to try out some new inspiration.

There was only time for a ground plan ($1/_2$" = 1' scale) and colour sketches; with the occasional model, but since the Scenic Artist would be working on the set with the carpenter, and any assistants the management could afford, there was not the need for elaborate technical drawings that are essential if the set is to be constructed in a workshop elsewhere.

The rapport that was established in many of the Repertories between the members of the back-stage staff was possible because there was no rigid compartmentalisation.

Equally the production of a satisfactory stage setting was not possible if there was not sufficient equipment – even a genius can only light one area at a time with only one spot light!

Ideally, one hopes for a unified achievement technically; but since directors vary in their interpretations of a play regarding the setting, what goes on within it acting wise, is of paramount importance.

A magnificent set will not save a production if the acting is poor; but good acting will compensate for a poor set. In many weekly Repertories this was the order of presentation.

The position today, seems to be that, whatever the aesthetic improvement may be judged to be, the costs of scenery, costumes, lighting, and sound, account for the largest part of the costs of production.

In 'The Theatre Industry' [1985] John Pick gives detailed accounts of the number of actors and other staff employed in 1952-53 in four subsidised companies, and the number employed in 1978-79.

			Actors	Other staff
Leatherhead	Theatre Club	1952/3	9	17
	Thorndike	1978/9	8	40
Salisbury	Playhouse	1958	11	23
		1978	15	53
Colchester	Repertory	1952/3	10	19
	Mercury	1978/9	10	41
Sheffield	Playhouse	1951/2	18	20
	Crucible	1978/9	27	130

Theatre historians are, and will be, immensely indebted to the patient research, and clear presentation, of theatre architecture, and theatre 'life', of Helen, and the late Richard Leacroft. This is especially true of 'Theatre and Playhouse' [1984]; the isometric drawings for this giving one such a clear picture of the dimensions of the many theatres considered; and indicating the whereabouts of the many additional areas to the main auditorium; as, for example, in the drawing of the Opera House, Leicester, where 'Stables for the Horses' is one area shown!

Richard and Helen met, and married, (Weekly Rep seemed to be a great 'marriage market') whilst working at the Theatre Royal, Leicester, at the beginning of the 1939-45 war. After the war Richard became the scenic Designer there, operating on the weekly change basis. I occupied a similar position there in 1952. Discussing those days we both agreed that the limitations of time and finance, were a stimulus to the imagination, insofar as we had to look at the materials available, and design a setting from these.

The three settings of mine (Illustrations 2.2, 2.3, and 2.4) for three weeks at the Theatre Royal, Leicester, 1952 are only of interest in that they illustrate three consecutive weeks. This means that Illustration 2.4 is painted on some of the flats seen in Illustration 2.2. All of the mouldings of the wood panels, and the architraving around the door, are painted effects. The buildings, seen across the courtyard, would be represented by a 16' x 3' flat on its side, with the battlements profiled on top.

The two settings by Richard Leacroft (Illustrations 2.5 and 2.6), show a more subtle use of lighting; and the multiple setting seems to have worked extremely well. Illustration 2.5 shows the New Leicester Theatre Co. in Anna Christie, February 1947; and Illustration 2.6 shows the New Leicester Theatre Co. in Desire under the Elms, November 1946; both at the Theatre Royal, Leicester.

The similar setting by Gardener Davies [2], done at Coventry [1931-40], shows the effect of area lighting; so much stressed by Adolph Appia', whose 'revolution' consisted, not so much in changes of auditorium and stage relationships, but in the awareness of the greater plasticity of electric light.

The notion that physical proximity to the actors means a more intense involvement with them, must be one of the strangest claims made, this century, by some theatre practitioners. It can work in reverse – if actors are only six feet away one may be conscious of some physical defect e.g., a wart on the neck, that distracts one; and if they are only six feet away from me then they are bound to be a long way from those sitting at the outer perimeter of the seating opposite. In 1932 Lee Simonson, in 'The Stage is Set' pointed out that, with regard to the Greek theatre "The worst seats at a Harvard football game correspond to being down at a performance of Aeschylus. Athenians ninety-one feet from a tragedy were in (front) the twenty-eighth row of seats. There were forty two tiers of seats behind them. Nevertheless the play at Athens was no more remote from its audience than a football game is from ours. For the Greek theatre succeeded in doing what every vital and popular theatre does: it did not thrust the players into the midst of the spectators; it thrust the theme of the play into the minds of its audience."

---

[1] 'Adventure in Repertory' [1948] A. Dyas, The Northampton Repertory Players.
[2] Gardener Davies was a producer of great talent, who met an untimely death by the collapse of a parapet on which he was sitting outside the Circle Bar of the theatre at Richmond (Surrey). He had previously done brilliant work in Coventry.

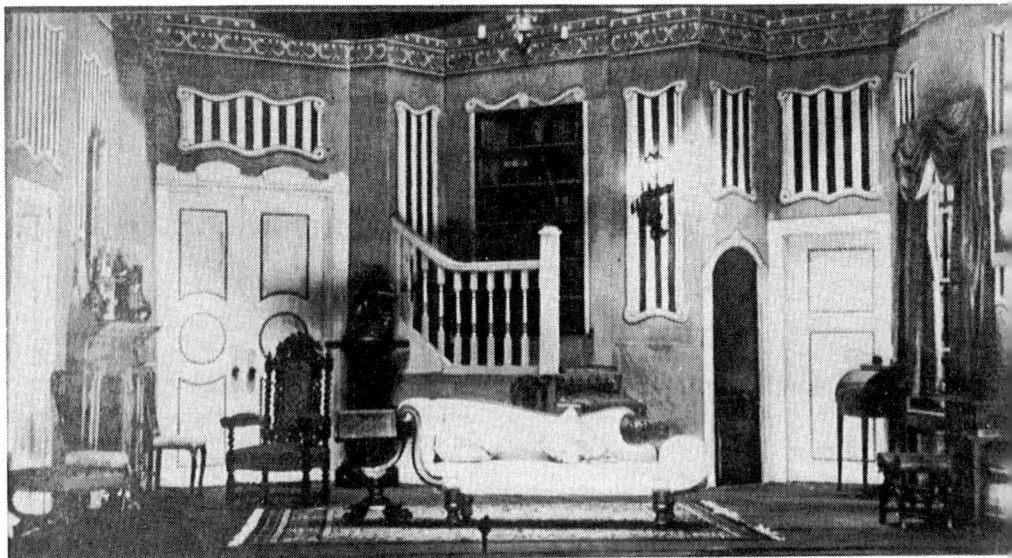

Illustration 2.2

Illustration 2.3

Illustration 2.4

Illustration 2.5

Illustration 2.6

Chapter 3

Plymouth [1915-35]

I am making 1915 my starting point in the history of Weekly Rep because, though there may have been companies, here and there, operating on a weekly change basis before the First World War, they would have been known as stock companies, and almost certainly working on a seasonal basis.

In 1915 a Repertory Company was founded in Plymouth by George S. King (always referred to as Geo. S. King) and this company played continuously, for twenty years, on a weekly change basis.

We are fortunate, in our starting point, in having the testimony of the distinguished drama critic and historian J. C. Trewin, to the value of the entertainment offered in this early Weekly Rep. He started his career as a drama critic at Plymouth in the 1920's. He writes, "For a moment I suggest that we leave the West End and travel down to the West Country port of Plymouth between its rivers and facing its sound. In 1950 the centre of Plymouth is a levelled, open plain. New roads have been driven through it, and the first buildings of a noble plan for reconstruction are beginning to rise. But Plymouth, in the middle twenties, before its centre was destroyed by the heaviest bombing the provinces knew, was a city of much charm, with its central streets coiled below the landward side of the Hoe's dominant bluff. For me it is always a fine noon in those ghost-streets. Bells chime the hour; there is a surge through the George Street narrows; sun glitters upon the limestone and upon certain pavements that made Hardy write of "the marble-streeted town". During the twenties the biggest theatre was part of Foulston's grand Ionic block, rightly called Royal, and containing theatre, hotel, and assembly rooms. In the middle thirties the theatre had ceased to pay. Soon, in place of the portico with its eight massive columns, a glory of the west, there rose a glum rubber-stamp cinema, the sort of building that might stand in any town, anywhere. (It survived the raids). Not far from the old Royal, at the corner of Princess square in the lawyers' quarter of the city, there was the tiny facade of the Repertory Theatre, earlier a Mechanics' Institute. George S. King, who opened this late in the year 1914, was a remarkable man. He had small resources, but he loved the stage; he was resolved to keep the Repertory going. Year in and out, he ran the place, doing everything between Shakespeare and Shaw, Our Flat and Monty's Flapper, upon a stage the size of a tilted tea-tray balanced upon a spiral stair. I have been in many smaller theatres – the 'Rep' held about 400 people – but I have never been in one that seemed to be so cramped, constructed on the scale of a doll's house. while other Repertories up the country were born and died, the little Plymouth theatre, curling itself round crisis after crisis, pressed on, piling up its number of productions and performances. It never pretended to compete in any way with such giants as Birmingham and Liverpool or, indeed, in matters of production and equipment, with such of the newer 'Reps' as Northampton, Hull, and Bristol. But it had its own blithe spirit; its sorely-tested weekly-change actors and its loyal playgoers – few but solid – loved the place sincerely."[1]

Geo. S. King kept the theatre open in spite of the financial difficulties encountered from time to time (not an unusual occurrence even in these days of subsidy) and when he died there was one central figure who inspired and motivated the other members of the company, and that was Bernard Copping (illustration 3.1), an actor who had been with Annie Horniman's Gaiety theatre company in Manchester.

He balanced a programme of the popular hits of the time with some Shakespeare and Shaw. Being an experienced and versatile actor he appeared in many of them himself.

Recalling those early days J.C. Trewin writes, "Alas, practically everybody has gone now but those weekly change years were sensational. Bernard Shaw took a special interest in the theatre during the early 1920's and allowed King to put on plays seldom seen elsewhere: Heartbreak House, for example, (Copping as Shotover), Captain Brassbound's Conversion, The Philanderer, and so on. Copping was an uncommonly subtle Shavian actor and would talk to me about the plays by the hour."[2]

George Bernard Shaw's connection with the Plymouth Rep is described in the book 'Shaw and Molly Tompkins'. The prodigious outpourings of Bernard Shaw, by means of letters and postcards, is now legendary. If you wrote to Shaw you got a reply.

In 1921 Molly Tompkins, a young wealthy American, came to England and audaciously introduced herself to Bernard Shaw at No. 10 Adelphi Terrace, London. Shaw took an interest in her, her husband Lawrence, and son Peter (who later edited the account of this friendship).

Expressing her desire to become an actress, Shaw advised her to go to the Royal Academy of Dramatic Art, at this time under the direction of Kenneth Barnes. This she did and her tutors included Claude Rains, best known now perhaps for his part in the much repeated film on T.V. 'Casablanca' starring Humphrey Bogart and Ingrid Bergman.

Another tutor was Mlle Gachet, who taught French and

Illustration 3.1 Bernard Copping

55

tutored her privately three times a week. It appears that Mlle Gachet after one of her private lessons, and over a cup of tea, inadvertently let slip the piece of information that the Plymouth Rep was wanting a leading lady, and the directors were considering two possible candidates to fulfil this role. Molly was not one of them.

She decided to make the trip to Plymouth and present herself to the manager. She phoned the theatre and spoke to him using the name of Mary Arthur. "Please don't give that job to anybody, until you have seen me. I am catching the first train down tonight. Please wait until I can talk to you. Yes, I know the director of the Academy has the giving of the job, but wouldn't you rather choose for yourself? No, no, he doesn't recommend me. On the contrary! But I will explain all that. I'm not sure about trains." I paused while he answered, then said goodnight and hung up.

"What did he say?" asked Laurence, anxiously.

"He said – and he has a nice slow lazy voice – "Now... now, there isn't that much rush. Take a morning train. The theatre won't run away and I'll be hereabouts, and I'll see you before I give the part."

So she caught an early train to Plymouth and she reports:

"George King, the manager of the Plymouth Repertory Company, was in his office when I got to the theatre; medium sized, hard-faced and a cigarette in one corner of his mouth which drifted smoke up past his eyes, he cocked his head and said:

"Well, Miss Arthur, what can you do?"

"Anything."

"Can you act?"

"I think so."

"What does Ken think?"

"Ken. Oh, you mean the director. He thinks I'm awful."

"Did you know he has the giving of this job?"

"Yes"

"How did you horn in?"

"I...er...heard you needed a leading lady."

"Can you be a leading lady?"

"I want to."

"Do you know what it means, acting every night, rehearsing every morning for the next week's play, studying your new lines whenever you get the chance?"

"Yes. No. Yes. It sounds lovely."

His eyes were very blue, his hair pleasantly grizzled. There was something clean and sweet about him, despite the rough face.

"What do you know?" he asked.

"Know?"

"Some piece. Can you say something?"

"Oh," I stuttered: "Gone to be married, gone to sign a truce, false blood to false blood joined." Then: "Come to my woman's breast and take my milk for gall, ye murdering ministers."

"Yeah. Anything but Shakespeare."

"They've made me do a lot of comedy, but I don't like it."

"You'll have to do plenty here."

"Then you're taking me?"

"Five pounds a week. Contract for one year. And you'll do what you're told. Now, I've got to write Ken what's burst. Get out. Rehearsal tomorrow at ten."

She promptly telegraphed Bernard Shaw and the following morning she began rehearsing the part of Kate Hardcastle in Goldsmith's 'She stoops to Conquer'. She comments, "While we read our lines, Mr. King, as he was known to his face, but whom everybody referred to affectionately as Mouldy Mike or just plain Mouldy, would pace up and down, a cigarette permanently drooping from his lips."

Later a telegram arrived from Shaw, "All this is first rate: you couldn't have done better. As far as I can guess without being on the spot the Plymouth Repertory is a gallant little enterprise; and I have always given Mr. King the licenses he asked for when my hands were not tied by other contracts..."

He continued to advise and encourage her. Her husband Laurence phoned her from London and spent most weekends with her in Plymouth. After a few weeks, however, she found that she could not cope with comedy; and though the other members of the company tried to help her the blow finally fell. Geo King felt that she was not an asset to his theatre and asked her to break her contract. This she agreed to do, and she relates:

"Shaw wrote demanding an explanation saying: "I do not for an instant believe you were sacked because you were no good. I want to know what happened."

He seemed to think that, in the time-honoured manner of the theatre, Mouldy had made improper advances and that I had walked out in a huff.

"Ask Mouldy" was all I could write him.

A few days later a letter arrived with an enclosure. The enclosure was in the large firm writing that I had only seen once before, on the contract Mouldy had signed. It said:

"Dear Mr. Shaw,

"Molly Tompkins: no, I do not think she's any good for the stage. I suppose I did worry her, but of course with only the best intentions. I felt it would be fatal to her chances to let her go sublimely on, thinking she was all right, when she was all wrong. Her voice is always – or nearly always – on top register: if it were possible to find a false emphasis, she'd do it: when she acted, it was with her head, I think, never with her heart. I thought finally, it was best for her to go – she was doing no good here."

"I shouldn't pass this on to you," Shaw added, "but I can't resist doing so."

"I hope he's satisfied," said Laurence dryly. "His ideas of actresses and managers seem to be culled from the movies."

Days drew into weeks. The only happy note in the sad affair was that because of his forthright answer about me, Shaw gave Mouldy the right to one of his plays."

We need to remind ourselves that in 1921 (the year when this took place) Annie Horniman decided to sell her Manchester Gaiety Theatre, and this left only the Birmingham and Liverpool Reps, plus a few stock companies – the main ones, in the latter category, being under the control of Alfred Denville, of whom more later.

There were few openings for aspiring actors and so it is not quite so surprising to find a R.A.D.A. student joining a Weekly Rep, especially as a leading lady.

The stock company differed from the Repertory company in that in the former actors had specific roles and always played these whereas in most Repertories all the members played as cast. So one week an actor had a big part and in the next a 'three liner'.

When the editor of the Plymouth local paper published my letter requesting 'memories and impressions' of this Rep I was not very hopeful of receiving any replies – but I received four – two of which were by octogenarians for whom those early Rep days still held a special place in their hearts and minds.

One correspondent, who was employed in a non-acting capacity wrote, "I was employed there from 1920 until my marriage in 1926, I was 19 years old in 1920 so it doesn't need a computer to tell you I shall never see 80 years again.

My retentive memory and the love I have for the years I spent there, it was such a happy place to work in, prompted me to write to you.

Now and again we did a Shaw play. We did 'Arms and the Man', 'You Never Can Tell', 'Pygmalion', etc. During the week that we did Shaw's 'Arms and the Man', Lord and Lady Mountbatten, who were on their honeymoon, were on their yacht in Plymouth Sound, and brought a party along to a performance.

The Rep Foyer where I was employed, had no bar, as such, I served the drinks from a very large sideboard. I was known as Tommy, my maiden name being Thompson.

Another little story, the late Sir Alan Cobham was, in the early twenties, the Daily Mirror Air Correspondent, he was engaged to one of our players – Gladys Lloyd – and spent quite a bit of his time in the Foyer. During the Easter of 1923 he asked to have a very large Easter egg passed up to Miss Lloyd, unfortunately it was broken. Mr. King, my boss, had it renewed, it was later presented and I well remember the large piece given to the staff."

Another correspondent worked there for the whole of its twenty year life. She wrote, "I was a member of the staff from when they opened on the Xmas 1915 until they closed in May 1935. I have many happy memories, having met so many nice people there. The theatre opened with a play called 'A Bunch of Violets' and every lady in the stalls and dress circle was presented with a bunch of violets on the opening night. The theatre had its ups and downs, especially during lent, when business was always bad, so they decided to close it down. But I must say we had some wonderful artists over the years. You may remember Richard Green of Robin Hood fame, he was born near the Plymouth Hoe, his father, also Richard Green was playing the lead at the Rep at that time which must be well over 60 years ago."

In the year [1935] when the Plymouth Rep finally closed 110 miles further north in Bristol, a young man named Ronald Russell, took over an ailing Repertory theatre and established The Rapier Players, a company that served that city well for 14 years as a Weekly Rep, and for another 14 years on a fortnightly basis. Much further north, in the historic city of York, another group of enthusiastic theatre goers were meeting to establish the York Citizens Theatre Company; and over the border, in Scotland, two young theatre enthusiasts – namely Marjorie Dence and David Steuart, with all the confidence of youth (and some financial backing from her father) founded the Perth Repertory Theatre. But before considering these enterprises we shall move to the Midlands and look at a Repertory company in the then mainly shoe manufacturing town of Northampton.

---

[1] 'Theatre since 1900' by J. C. Trewin [1950].
[2] Letter to author.

Illustration 3.2 Plymouth Rep [1915-35]

Chapter 4

Northampton [1927-57]

I have indicated that the initial move in forming the Repertory companies was one of three ways – either an existing owner of a theatre, e.g. Leo Salberg: or a private patron such as Barry Jackson or Miss Horniman, purchased, or built, a theatre and provided the initial finance to start it off. Thirdly, an interested group of people, who were dissatisfied with the existing theatre fare, formed a syndicate and jointly provided the finance to start the project.

This was the position at Northampton in 1927 and we are fortunate in having a record of the subsequent twenty years in 'Adventure in Repertory' by Aubrey Dyas. This is an account of the first 20 years [1927-48] of the Northampton Repertory company, and it contains the lists of plays produced, averaging 45 a year; and lists of the players for each year. It has a foreword by J. B. Priestley, which helps to put the Repertory movement in a better perspective. Priestley realised that what Northampton had to offer was undoubtedly better than no theatre at all.

The development of the Northampton Repertory is worth looking at in more detail, not only because we have the reliable evidence of A. Dyas, but because it was typical of some of the Repertories that emerged during the twenties and thirties.

Amongst the instigators of the move to found a Repertory company in Northampton were the editors of the two local newspapers namely 'The Northampton Independent' and 'The Northampton Echo'.

Members of the Rotary Club showed interest in the project and, besides the two editors mentioned, there were three other people, with business and cultural interests in Northampton, who formed the nuclei of the new movement.

The Mayor of Northampton called a public meeting to discuss the possibility of launching a repertory theatre in the town.

After many meetings and much discussion; and in spite of the prophets of doom who forecast that 'it wouldn't last four months', there was sufficient support to justify the founding body looking for a theatre.

The Opera House, which seated 850 seemed the obvious choice, and the stage of which had presented many famous players and performers amongst whom were Sir Henry Irving, Ellen Terry, Edward Compton, and Virginia Bateman, Sir Charles Wyndham, Mary Moore, Osmund Tearle, Kitty Loftus, Wilson Barrett, Genevieve Ward, Laurence Irving, Fred Terry and Julia Neilson, Sir Frank Benson, 'Little Tich', Sir John Martin Harvey, Frank Curzon, Sir Seymour Hicks, and Charlie Chaplin. On one visit of the Carl Rosa Opera Company, the orchestra was conducted by Sir Henry Wood. But the place was due to be demolished. Could they save it from destruction?

Eventually, a company known as 'Northampton Repertory Players Limited' was formed with a capital of £2,000 divided into 2,000 ordinary shares of £1 each.

There is one observation by A. Dyas regarding this initial effort that is worth quoting in full. Rightly, or wrongly, no one expected money, to maintain this theatrical enterprise, to come from any public funds. He writes – "Although the scheme to establish a repertory theatre received the official blessing of the Mayor, it will be observed that there was no suggestion that it should be a civic theatre. Such a proposition would probably have been regarded as revolutionary. In the English official mind, the theatre is not considered among the civic assets of the community. Museums, art galleries, and public libraries are permissible burdens for the rate payers, but not the living theatre. In this respect, of course, Northampton does not differ from any other English town or city."

A company of eleven players, all with professional status was engaged, amongst whom was the actor Clifton James, who later was to play an important role as a decoy to Field Marshall Montgomery, when the authorities wanted the Germans to believe that he was somewhere other than where he was!

The producer chosen was Mr. Max Jerome who had helped to lay the foundations of the high standard of dramatic art offered by the Little Theatre, Bristol. He had also been a member of Sir Frank Benson's company.

It was in keeping with the spirit of the times that the supporters of the Repertory Company formed themselves into the Northampton Playgoers Association. There was no Arts

Council to appeal to for funds – they knew that if the Repertory was to pay its way it would need regular support and a regular income.

In 1927 petrol was 1s. 1$\frac{1}{2}$d a gallon, sheets 12s. 6d a pair, port 3s. 6d a bottle, and coal 45s. a ton. Although nearing their sudden demise, silent films were in vogue, and amongst others the most famous were Rudolph Valentino, Harold Lloyd, Gloria Swanson and Buster Keeton.

For the opening play the directors chose Sir Arthur Pinero's 'His House in Order' – a strong play with a broad appeal.

The majority of theatre personnel outside of Northampton, at that time, took a lively interest in what was going on in the provincial theatre and Dyas reports that "A host of felicitations were received by the company, including a gracious and encouraging message from Sir Barry Jackson. "I congratulate Northampton upon its enterprise" he wrote, "and I wish the venture every success.""

This last remark is significant in showing that, though they may have been a little sceptical about the quality of the productions presented on a twice nightly, change weekly basis, those who were trying to establish good repertory companies gave encouragement to any enterprise in this direction.

After all – if a theatre is open and functioning efforts can be made to improve the standard of performances.

The settings for the initial productions were done by Charles Maynard – the following year was to see this position taken up by Tom Osborne Robinson – one of the most significant characters in the history of weekly repertory, or for that matter, theatre generally.

In spite of the scoffers and 'dismal Desmonds' who from the beginning prophesised failure, the Northampton Repertory Company managed to survive and to build up a regular clientele.

In 1928, the Board of Directors appointed Herbert Prentice as the producer. He stayed with the company for four years producing 200 plays before being asked by Sir Barry Jackson to produce at the Birmingham Repertory Theatre. Herbert Prentice played a leading part in founding the Sheffield Repertory Theatre where he worked, as a producer, for seven years.

On the strength of his work here he was asked by another wealthy young theatre enthusiast, namely Terence Gray, to produce at his Festival Theatre in Cambridge.

This he did for three years, presenting work of a high acting standard, but eventually suffering from Gray's emphasis on the aesthetic importance above all other considerations – again Aubrey Dyas "A repertory theatre needs to be conducted with the utmost vigilance and foresight, and the fate of the Cambridge Festival Theatre illustrates what happens when these qualities are lacking. You see, Terence Gray was a brilliant dilettante in whose productions special emphasis was placed upon the staging. Invariably, the settings had amazing beauty of colour and line but were characterised by eccentricity and marred by quaint conceits. Time and again this stressing of inessentials tended to obscure the meaning of the play itself. "The meaning doesn't matter," Gray would say. "A theatre is purely aesthetic art." But gorgeous trappings do not make a play. After all, although we have the facilities for elaborate mounting and subtle lighting today, such as were unknown to Shakespeare, "the play's the thing" still. Not surprisingly the public tired of Gray's concentration on pictorial qualities of a production to the detriment of the play itself; doubtless they found the mechanical delights of the cinema more vital and satisfying, and in 1933 the Cambridge Festival Theatre was forced to close its doors."

Sir Barry Jackson's choice of H. Prentice to work at the Birmingham Repertory Theatre is indicative of his high regard for his work at Northampton and elsewhere.

The point I wish to stress to those who may be sceptical about the standard of acting and presentation in weekly repertory is, that at Northampton, for four years at least, a high standard was maintained, and there is substantial evidence to show that other weekly repertories achieved comparable standards of acting.

On the occasion of the Annual Conference of the British Drama League on 25 October, 1929, being held in Northampton, the company produced 'The Queen was in the Parlour', the first production of a play by the then twenty-nine year old Noel Coward.

"The delegates, who came from all parts of the country and included the Rt. Hon. Earl of Lytton, K. G., Prof. Gilbert Murray, O.M., and Mr. Geoffrey Whitworth, were unanimous in their praise of the acting, the astute production of Herbert Prentice, and the beautiful settings of Osborne Robinson, who once again excelled himself. Indeed, this performance was a triumph for all concerned and served to demonstrate to the visitors the high standard of work accomplished by this youthful Repertory Theatre."

In 1930 we find Bernard Shaw visiting Northampton to see his friends Mr. and Mrs. Banister-Lowke who managed to persuade Shaw to grant permission for the Northampton Repertory players to perform 'Fanny's First Play'.

In this same year Sir Barry Jackson visited the theatre and saw 'A Hundred Years Old' by Quintero; and afterwards praised the performance and interpretation of this Spanish comedy, which he preferred to the West End production.

The drama critics of the main national newspapers rarely ventured beyond the theatre of London's West End; but in 1933 the Conference of Repertory Theatres Association held their annual meeting at Northampton and W. A. Darlington, the critic of the Daily Telegraph wrote "Today I have paid a visit to Northampton's excellently run Repertory Theatre, and have seen a performance of Louis N. Parker's The Cardinal, which, for directness of method and clearness of speaking, would give points to many more pretentious productions." After dealing with the method of work at the Repertory Theatre, Mr. Darlington remarked, "The work done by the producer and the company at the Northampton Theatre is nothing short of heroic," and then concluded, "The people of Northampton have a real live theatre in their midst. I hope they know their luck.""

I doubt if there is a Repertory Company today, even with subsidy, that could afford to mount a production in celebration of the anniversary of the birth of a distinguished local literary figure; but in 1935 we find Bladon Peake the then Producer, instituting an annual Dryden festival which won for the Repertory Theatre high repute among discerning critics and playgoers. John Dryden, who was born at the rectory of Aldwincle All Saints, between Thrapston and Oundle, on 9 August, 1631, is the only dramatist Northampton can claim.

'Marriage à la Mode', chosen for the first festival, aroused widespread interest. A production of Dryden's best comedy, first acted in May 1672, was hailed as an event of considerable literary and dramatic importance to all theatre lovers. This witty, satirical comedy proved a wise choice and besides meeting with instantaneous response from the public, received enthusiastic notices in the national newspapers and reviews. For instance the New Statesman declared: "High praise must be awarded to Mr. Osborne Robinson for his delightful black and white permanent setting and gay costumes. The producer, Mr. Bladon Peake, confronted with a heavy task, wisely decided to concentrate on pace and the comedy went with a swing throughout."

Sir Archibald Flower, chairman of the governors of the Shakespeare Memorial Theatre, Stratford-on-Avon, and Mr. B. Iden Payne, the producer, who were among the many distinguished visitors, *expressed their amazement that a production of such quality could be achieved in such a short time. They voiced their admiration for the actors who so readily assumed the heroic mould, and the excellent work of Mr. Peake and Mr. Robinson.*

'The Spanish Friar' was chosen for the second Dryden Festival; and in 1937 they chose 'Sir Martin Marr-All'. This was considered to be a significant and praiseworthy achievement which received wide commendation including a half column notice in both The Times and the Daily Telegraph. Graham Greene, then the drama critic of The Spectator wrote "The production at Northampton deserves high praise."

"Mr. Peake's production is forthright, definite, and decisively in the vein of Restoration farce", remarked The Times critic, "Mr. Osborne Robinson who designed the sets, is also responsible for an extraordinary gay wardrobe, not slavishly restricted in style, but always favouring the right period under a generous imaginative elaboration". The Daily Telegraph was even more eulogistic, it said, "Osborne Robinson's dresses are amusing and delightful enough to make the artiste's reputation in a night: if London could see them. The material is slipper felt, and the total cost of the magnificent show is said to have been £50".

If there was a place in the Guinness Book of Records for the performance of multiple assignments in one day in the history of the theatre; then 3 January, 1934, would be a day well to the fore amongst the claimants. On this day the Repertory company –

rehearsed Bull Dog Drummond,

played a matinee of Jack and the Beanstalk (with a young actor named Errol Flynn as Prince Donzil), gave two evening performances of Sweet Lavender, broadcast the one-acter, The Dear Departed.

I think 'heroic' is the best word to sum up this day's work.

Those who think that Weekly Repertory performances must have been ad-libbed and improvised can have a field day imaginatively picturing the players getting through this particular one!

Or, maybe, they might concede that 'all things are possible' to those who are committed to making a success of their combined efforts.

One could not, starting from scratch, expect a group of actors today to do what this group did on this particular day in 1934.

But if we remember that most of these people had worked together for two or three years; were disciplined to memorising lines quickly, and had acquired the natural awareness of each others strengths and weaknesses, then it is easier to accept.

During Robert Young's directorship the Company fielded a cricket eleven – he was opposed "to all work and no play"! A. Dyas reports "Both Mr. Young and Mr. Roberts were trained in the right school, that of Sir Frank Benson, one of the keenest sportsmen in the theatrical profession, who got his blue for the three miles at Oxford. His encouragement of his Company to play games led to a host of fables about sport in the Benson Company. It was said Sir Frank used to advertise: "wanted a Laertes and centre-forward" and "wanted a good bowler for Roderigo."

Chapter 5

Tom Osborne Robinson O.B.E.

I now wish to consider the achievement of the man who helped to make Northampton Repertory, for its 30 years as a Weekly Repertory, and beyond, such a success. Rowell and Jackson [1984] express surprise that until the publication of their book there had been no sustained account of the British Repertory movement, and with the exception of J. Elsom's 'Theatre Outside of London' [1971], which deals mainly with theatre since 1960, we have to go back to Cecil Chisholm's [1934] 'Repertory' for an interesting survey of Repertory covering the early years. It seems remarkable that in these two accounts, separated by a span of 50 years, there is an illustration of a stage design by Tom Robinson, as he was, and still is, affectionately referred to by the many who knew him.

The early one is of a design for 'Twelfth Night' and the later for a Northampton Repertory production entitled 'Northampton Harlequinade' produced by Nugent Monck.

If one had to name one's outstanding person of the theatre through the ages, no doubt the ensuing answers would vary according to one's own particular interest in the theatre. Many would regard the works of Shakespeare, or Bernard Shaw, as singularly outstanding achievements; Henry Irving and Laurence Olivier as two actors who have performed with distinction. There have been outstanding efforts in the field of design, though perhaps it would be easier to name, from this century, one's top ten, and certainly mine would include Tom Osborne Robinson.

But I doubt if more than a few of today's theatre personnel would be aware of his extraordinary achievement.

As I have mentioned, he began with the Northampton Repertory company in 1928.

One of three children he was born in 1904.

His father, in partnership with his brother, set up a cycle business in Northampton, not only selling them but also making them. Later, they began making motorcycles and then motor cars.

Tom's brother Colin, in an interesting memoir published after his death in 1976, records that his first artistic efforts were in connection with shows put on at the local Baptist church, which was just 'up the road' and at which their parents were regular attenders. "So the ever open doors of Sunday School buildings provided refuge, not only for children, but also for young people and occasionally for the whole family. Band of Hope, magic lantern shows, jumble sales, sales of work, youth organisations, parties and social evenings and 'threepenny

Illustration 5.1 Tom Osborne Robinson

hops' and choir practice, and concerts, and Sunday School concerts, and many other events. As the years went by and we became ever more involved, there weren't many evenings when one or more of the Robinson family wasn't 'up the road'.

It was the last item on that list of activities which gave Tom an opportunity to use his obvious developing artistic talent. Mother delighted in producing children's operettas, usually involving fairies and pixies. These required succession of forest glades and fairy dells and grottoes. The budding scenic designer worked wonders with next to nothing and with an exuberance unusual in a boy. Then came more serious efforts requiring costumes (designed by Osborne Robinson) and Christmas Tableaux (dressed by Osborne Robinson) and a pantomime (created by Osborne Robinson)."

His formal education began at a small private school run by two spinster sisters.

He later went to the Grammar School but by that time Tom's obsession with art was well developed to the exclusion of all else – early indications of that single-mindedness of purpose which was to become his principle characteristic.

The Headmaster, a Mr. Reynolds, obviously had little enthusiasm for art and an almost derisive dislike of any pupil who had an excessive interest in it.

The decisive experience for Tom was in 1921 when he was taken by his father on a trip to London, finishing up at the Alhambra Theatre to see Diaghilev's Russian ballet 'The Sleeping Princess' with decor and costumes by Bakst. He later recorded – "... it was a revelation which revolutionised my whole attitude to life. I knew then that nothing would stop me from designing scenery and costumes. I knew also that school was an utter waste of time for me and I resolved not even to attempt to learn."

He left the school before completing the usual period set in those days and the end of term leave taking provided the final indignity with the usual handshake by the 'Head' and polite enquiry as to future career. Again I quote "When Reynolds asked about my future I told him bluntly that my only ambition was to go in for Art. His sarcasm and laughter burned deep into my memory for years afterwards. Going in for Art? Surely a blot on the school's escutcheon?"

Understandably this was a blow to his parents who to some

extent shared the Head's distrust of Art as a career. In their book Art was associated with the notion of living (or more likely starving) in an attic with successions of undesirable women.

Tom solved his own problem by becoming an 'apprentice' commercial artist. Starting salary? Five shillings a week!

Long working days in the business studio, evenings spent at the Northampton School of Art in Abington Street, everything looked at from the point of view of colour, form and design, all stored away in memory or in sketch books for future use when the opportunity arose. A life completely devoted to his one consuming interest. Nothing else mattered.

Six years learning that in business the customer is always right and that the artist, however creative, must always comply. But six years, also, of fruitful work at the Art School where his genius was recognised and encouraged by the then principal, the late Lewis Duckett, to whom several budding artists of that time had reason to be grateful for his expert guidance.

In 1926 he was awarded the Travelling Scholarship for two weeks in Paris. But the decisive event that was to start him on his long theatrical career happened in 1928 when during preparations for John Drinkwater's play, 'Mary Stuart' with settings half completed, the scene painter downed tools and walked out. This was Tom's opportunity to gain entrance to the work he aspired to do. He was asked to finish the work. This he did – the curtain went up on time and the job was his for the taking.

Lou Warwick, a friend of Tom, wrote in a foreword to Colin Robinson's memoir "From then on and for close on half a century he was a part of the Repertory miracle. He always had to have at least three plays on his mind at one and the same time – the one on stage, the next one for which he was preparing and the one beyond that which, at that point, would probably be but a few ideas in his fertile mind. And, staggering as it may now seem in these days of three-week shows, for the greater part of his time as designer it was a weekly miracle.

Even to get weekly shows on stage at all was a feat in itself for all concerned but, under those pressures, to produce such sets that almost all were memorable and seemed inspired.... well, that is the product of dedicated genius."

Bryan Douglas, who worked with Tom Robinson for 20 years, and built most of his sets after 1957 and, fortunately, photographed most of them, told me that Tom lived quite near the theatre, and appeared to survive on a constant brew of soup which he kept going – "He had this large saucepan and he would throw in bits of meat and vegetables – and this was his main source of nourishment."

There is no suggestion ever of a man complaining that he had so little time in which to prepare his work. On the contrary he seemed to thrive on the constant challenge of new work. He was 'married to his work' and enjoyed the freedom from concern with the raising of a family; a condition that has made working in the theatre extremely difficult, and one of the reasons why many of the 95% who have started work in theatre have given up and sought more regular work elsewhere.

In 1951 I was working, as the Scenic Artist, for a touring company in the north of England, and he was asked by the producer to design the sets and costumes for 'Macbeth'. These duly arrived – a ground plan and colour sketches, plus costume designs.

As if designing and producing a set for a play each week was not enough, we find him, in 1955, meeting with Roy Gentry, who later became the display manager for Liberty & Co. This was the beginning of a friendship that lasted until Tom's death in 1976. Roy Gentry comments,

"I first met Tom Osborne Robinson in the crush bar at Covent Garden in 1955. In the course of conversation, he discovered I worked in display at Liberty. He was designing the set for 'Ring Round the Moon'. He asked me if it might be possible to borrow some very large silk lanterns we were using in the windows, for his set. This I was able to arrange and later at Christmas he sent me a card he had designed himself.

I became display manager shortly afterwards, and when thinking about the first Christmas windows I would be responsible for in 1957, I remembered his card. I wrote, asking him if it would be possible to use 'The Spirit of Christmas' figure, from his card, in my windows. This came to pass and so began a collaboration and friendship that I valued greatly.

We had recently had a new entrance to the store that year and I remember I persuaded him to come along one cold, foggy November Sunday, and paint the same figure on the wall of the entrance.

For Christmas 1962 he came up with the three kings idea. He

designed each face and headdress differently and these were made in paper cloth in gold, silver, and copper.

For Christmas 1969 I asked him to design sets of masks and headdresses e.g. ballet, music and drama; the four seasons and old Father Time, the four elements etc.

For Christmas 1971, I turned the length of the Regent Street windows into one long advent calendar. I asked Tom if he could undertake the painting of the 45 yard run of blockboard panels in winter scenes, in the style of the Dutch masters. The panels were all transported to Northampton and he and his assistant painted them over a period of weeks.

They were an enormous success and people would spend ages wandering the length of the frontage and sometimes come again and still find some little incident or character in the panorama they had missed before.

The last windows he did for me were for Christmas 1972, which featured panels cut into three, with figures painted on them, in the style of childrens books, where you get amusing interposition of parts of characters when turning only one of the sections.

Tom was the kindest of men, always ready to help and encourage others and able to convey his love of beauty to others, and completely selfless. It was through him I paid my first visit to Venice, a city that he loved above all others and which he visited more than twenty times, I believe.

Certainly knowing him greatly enriched my life and I am sure there are very many people who would say the same."

Tom spent three vacations working in American Universities. The following are two of the responses to my enquiries regarding his work there. The first was 1962-3.

Joseph Wright, who is now Professor Emeritus of Drama at Vanderbilt University, Nashville, Tennessee, commented "Tom taught a course in Scene Design and two sections of our course, 'Fundamentals of Theatre'. Now, 27 years later, I don't recall his exact schedule; but I believe he taught 'Fundamentals' in the Fall Semester and the other two in the Spring Semester. He was responsible for all design and technical direction.

Tom's superb artistry and his capacity for hard work were not strange or new. I had the privilege of a season's association with him at Northampton in 1953-4. He designed 11 productions which I directed. You know the quality of his work. I can add

❏ Four Settings by Tom Osborne Robinson

Illustration 5.2 'Tobias and the Angel' [1939]

Illustration 5.3 'The Marquise' [1946]

Illustration 5.4 'Androcles and the Lion' [1943]

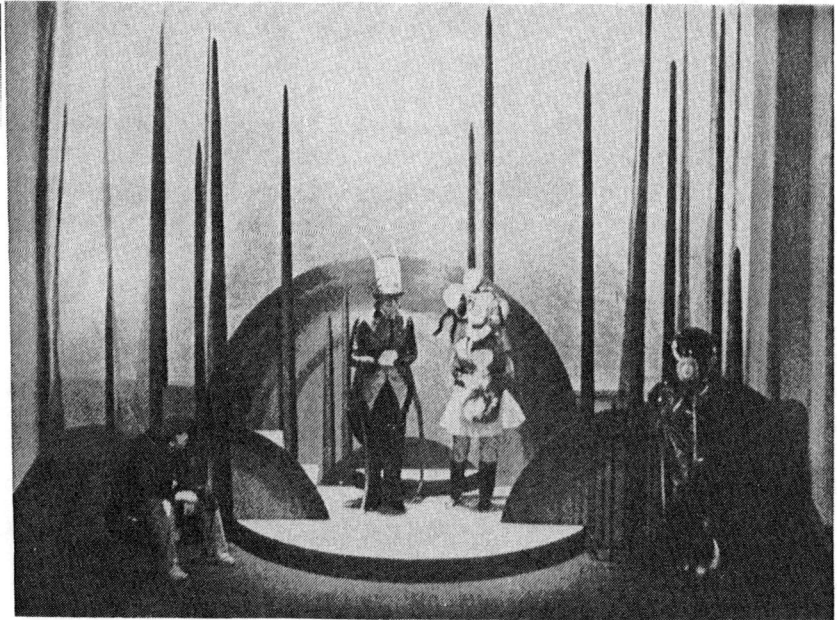

Illustration 5.5 'The Insect Play' [1938]

nothing to all that has been said. You will not be surprised to learn that he was beloved by his students both in the courses and in the theatre.

That 1962-3 season with Tom was my last as an active director; I could not have been more pleased. We did an original play, an opera, and The Merchant of Venice. Tom also supervised the technical work for a full-length production by one of my directing students. All this plus a series of one-acts directed by our students combined to make this a vastly rewarding season.

We were co-hosts that year for the annual meeting of the Southeastern Theatre Conference. Our contribution to the entertainment schedule was The Merchant of Venice. The reception was stunning. Nashville has not seen a more visually appealing production".

Douglas Russell, Professor of Drama at Stanford University, California, wrote "My wife and I had a wonderful visit with him in Northampton in 1970, and a memorable trip through the National Gallery with Tom as art guide. In the spring of 1971 Tom came to visit us in Vienna, where I was teaching Stanford students and we went to many Viennese sites. He also gave a marvellous lecture to the Stanford students on the Art of Venice. His memory for the exact placement of every painting he had ever seen was phenomenal. At Stanford Tom designed settings for a number of productions, as well as posters to be used in productions. Tom scoured bookstores, antique markets, small galleries and many art studios, looking for items for his collections and those of the Northampton Gallery. He also took many trips – one all the way to the Mayan ruins in Mexico; and all of us here felt he was a walking demonstration of how knowledgeable and multi-interested a good theatre designer could be. He was MR. ARTS here at Stanford – a pied piper who captured everyones' interest in all the visual arts. We felt a real vacancy when he left to return to England."

It has been suggested that, perhaps, he carried on too long – he was 70 years old when he eventually retired. This may have been the case; but the letter, published in the Northampton Chronicle & Echo in 1975, and signed by several eminent people associated with the arts, indicates the respect and gratitude there was for him far beyond the town which he served so well.

Amongst the 100 signatories we find the names of John Bury, then the Head of Design at the National Theatre; Sir Roy Strong, Sir Norman Reid, Dr. Edmund Rubbra, Dr. Richard Southern, J. L. Carr, and Sir Sacheverell Sitwell, who wrote "Osborne Robinson is among the most distinguished living artists of the theatre."

Whereas the work of Paul Shelving at Birmingham Rep, and George Harris at Liverpool, is justly praised, there is no doubt, in my mind, that Tom Robinson was second to none.

Thomas Osborne Robinson, O.B.E.

1921 (Aged 17) 'saw Diaghilev's Russian Ballet, The Sleeping Princess', with Bakst decor and costumes. This was a revelation which revolutionised my whole attitude to life. I knew then that nothing would stop me from designing scenery and costumes ...'

1922-8 Commercial artist.

1926 Awarded Art School travelling scholarship £10 for two weeks in Paris.

1928-75 Scenic designer and later Head of Design for Northampton Repertory Theatre.

Estimated output of more than 3,000 sets and many thousands of costumes.

1937 Settings and costumes for Old Vic 'Hamlet', produced by Tyrone Guthric, with Laurence Olivier.

1937 Settings and costumes for Old Vic 'Hamlet', staged in Elsinore Castle, Denmark.

1937 Settings and costumes for Old Vic 'Richard III'. Emlyn Williams as Richard.

1937 Offer by Lillian Bayliss of permanent job as scene painter and designer at Old Vic Theatre. Not accepted.

1938 Settings and costumes for Stratford 'Macbeth'.

1947 Settings and costumes for Stratford Christmas production 'Alice in Wonderland'.

1947 Settings and costumes for Stratford 'As You Like It'.

1952 Costumes for Century Theatre's first production 'Othello'.

1952 Costumes for Royal Masque, performed before Princess Elizabeth on the occasion of receiving Oxford University honours.

1952 Settings for 'Merry Wives of Windsor' and 'Saint Joan' for New Zealand.

1954 Settings for 'Midsummer Night's Dream' Vanderbilt University, Tennessee.

1962/3 Guest Lecturer in Drama and Design, Vanderbilt University. Designed their productions of 'Merchant of Venice' and 'Barber of Seville' and also outdoor production of 'Mikado'.

1965 Texas, designed and executed large mural 'Signing of Magna Carta' and for Academy of Freedom, Howard Payne College, awarded Honorary 1968 Freedom of State of Texas.

1968 Awarded Arts Council Bursary for Travel and Theatre Study in Central Europe.

1969/70 Guest Lecturer and designer at Stanford University, California.

1969 Awarded O.B.E. for Services to Arts.

1973 Grosvenor Centre, Northampton, Commissioned to design and execute murals depicting scenes from local history. (not completed).

Member of Northampton Town and County Arts Society, from 1923 till his death. Hon. Secretary 1945-52. President 1955-7.

Founder member of Friends of Northampton Museums and Art Gallery from 1955. Its Chairman from then until his death.

Chairman of Association of Stage Designers 1949-51.

Member of Arts Council Drama Panel 1967-9.

Involved in many local activities for encouragement of arts.

Trained students at Northampton Museums and Art Gallery.

Presented his Life-time's collection of 3,500 posters to Northampton College of Art.

Chapter 6

Manchester (Rusholme) [1923-40]

There is a point in Peter Street, Manchester, where one can stand and, imaginatively, conjure up the ghosts of many characters associated with the musical and theatrical history of this city, and indirectly, of this country.

Quite often, after having spent a morning going through copies of the then Manchester Guardian in search of this or that item of fact, or opinion, relating to my subject matter, I would venture to the Berni bar, in Peter Street, for a pint and a sandwich. Then, feeling refreshed, I would return to the street and, not wishing immediately to return to the Central Library, stand on the pavement and let my thoughts centre around the past associations of the buildings one can see from this position.

Away to my extreme left is the Central Library – the repository of records of all kinds of information and open to all kinds of people, who hope to find the answers to their questions.

Across the road, opposite the Central Library, there stands the massive red brick building of the Midland Hotel. Almost everyone of importance, who visited Manchester, stayed at the Midland.

Behind me, on the wall of new business premises, there is a circular plaque on which it states:

THE SITE OF
THE GAIETY THEATRE
DIRECTED BY
MISS A. E. HORNIMAN
1908-1921

This was the home of the first provincial Repertory company and I like to think that, when I am having my glass of beer downstairs in the Berni Inn, I am sitting in the stalls of the

Gaiety Theatre – on stage I hear the full 'bloom and boom' of that remarkable character Sybil Thorndyke, who did so much to encourage Repertory (including some weekly change ones) throughout her long life and partnership with Lewis Casson.

If, in imagination, I go back further in time to when the Gaiety was the Comedy Theatre and the home of Music Hall, I can spot a young lad, up in the gallery, selling chocolates; having spent the morning in the self same library where, 70 years later, I find myself. He was there because, having lost his job at a printers, and afraid to tell his mother and grand parents, with whom he was living, he would walk the three miles into Manchester at the same time as was previously required to get him to the printworks, and then walk around Manchester, until the doors of the Central Library were opened, and he was admitted into that world of concentrated wit and wisdom (not to mention Wisden!) that he was to add to so richly. His name was Neville Cardus.

Reflecting on those days, many years after, when he was a recognised writer on cricket and music he recalled the richness of cultural life in Manchester at the turn of the century. He writes, "I remember a week in Manchester when a new play by Galsworthy was given at the Gaiety Theatre on Monday; on Tuesday there was a concert of the Brodsky Quartet; on Wednesday a matinee by Rejane; on Thursday a Halle Concert, with Richter and Busoni, and on Friday a production of Ibsen's Ghosts, connived in camera; for Ghosts was then a banned play in England." [1]

He did not however wholly share the mood of earnestness and high aspirations of the Manchester intelligentsia who went to the Gaiety Theatre for uplift.

Across the road one can see the Theatre Royal; now mainly the venue for Disco; but at the time of Cardus' youth it was one of the theatres housing the touring companies of, amongst others, Beerbohm Tree and Henry Irving. These productions were lavish in scenic display and less pretentious in cerebral exercise, but displaying colour and personality.

Cardus writes: "The intelligentsia of Manchester, shepherded by Montague, went knowingly and in droves to these dreary slices of life; the same people attended surreptitiouslly on Beerbohm Tree across the way at the Theatre Royal; perhaps, like myself they kept to themselves their feeling that after all there is something to be said for personality." [2]

The then Manchester Guardian, under C. P. Scott, was rich in critics of the Arts: Ernest Newman and Sam Langford on music: Alan Monkhouse, C. E. Montague and James Agate on theatre. The latter, throughout his life, seemed to display a dislike of 'intellectuals' – though he himself was possessed of no mean intelligence, and most later critics are agreed in saying that he was a good judge of acting. When Annie Horniman died in 1937 he wrote a tribute to her and also reflected on those days at the Gaiety. He writes, "A lot of nonsense has been and will be written about Manchester's failure to support the venture at the Gaiety Theatre. The truth of the matter is that the Gaiety, after a brave start, let down Manchester badly. At the beginning, with managers like Iden Payne, Basil Dean, and Lewis Casson, and players like Miss Darragh, Sybil Thorndike, and Henry Austin, all went grandly. Later, managers of lesser calibre were engaged, the plays became steadily drearier, and the players more purposefully amateur. Now, perhaps, it may be said that there never was a Manchester school of drama, but only an odd dramatist or two who happened to be born or to live in Manchester. Stanley Houghton's 'Hindle Wakes' was a bright flash in what turned out to be a very small pan, and Harold Brighouse never followed up 'Hobson's Choice'. The only first-class work of the so-called Manchester school was Allan Monkhouse's 'Mary Broome'. But still the notion that there could be such a school persisted, as nobody knows better than I do. (I functioned as a dramatic critic on the staff of the M. G. all through this very period). Time after time the curtain would go up on a Welsh dresser and a kitchen table with Sybil weeping in frustration. Sometimes the dresser would be to the left, sometimes to the right. But the table and Sybil were constant.

Now consider what happened at the Gaiety. By stripping the gold paint and all garish appurtenances, and substituting a decor of unrelieved white, the place was made as much like a schoolroom and as little like a theatre as possible. There was no drink licence, but only the horrid spectacle of intellectuals consuming cocoa. No orchestra, and in the intervals pale young men, who had not gone out to drink cocoa, nodded glumly to one another across Professor Herford's beard." [3]

Across the road, and to my right, I can see the classical portico of the Free Trade Hall, the present home of the Halle, and offering music to an audience of people who, during the day will be occupied in a variety of situations, but who come together to share the experience of listening to a great orchestra.

I'm sure that we all have recollections, either from our own experience, or from literature, that evoke a pleasant chuckle, and one of mine is induced by the imaginative picturing of the young N. Cardus walking, terrier like, on the heels of Sam Langford and Ernest Newman (two of the Manchester Guardian's distinguished music critics) from the Free Trade Hall to the Midland Hotel, in the hope of hearing that one remark that would encapsulate and explain the whole experience of music – but not tonight – they turn into the welcoming warmth of the Midland Hotel, and Neville must make his way back to his solitary digs – but I'm sure, not entirely empty-minded.

I chuckle over O'Casey's Fluther Good boasting to Nora "I hit a man last week and he's still falling...!" – he was last seen staggering down O'Connell Street backwarding straight for the river Liffey!

(God only knows how many Fluther Goods, scared stiff, must have staggered out of the ruins of Beirut during the last ten years on some errand of mercy).

This preamble is intended to set the scene of my next Weekly Rep venue, namely the Manchester (Rusholme) Repertory Co. who occupied a theatre in Rusholme not far from the birth place of N. Cardus. The time was 1923-1940. It is also intended to highlight the general dismissal of any mention of Weekly Rep, by some theatre historians, as being not worthy of their consideration.

There were not sufficient members of the Manchester public interested in A. Horniman's Gaiety theatre to keep it going and, eventually, she sold it and it became a cinema. There is a sad, but not tragic, comment on this good lady in the book by that delightful gourmet snob John Fothergill entitled 'An Innkeeper's Diary'. He writes in 1927, "Staying here is Miss Horniman, founder of the Manchester Repertory Theatre; she who was one of the modern women of the world, now the very dearest old maid. The cigarette in a holder, but only aftermeals, is all that remains of her hardihood."

We have clear evidence of the origin of many of the Reps – Sheffield and York for example – but there is little evidence to show just how the Rusholme Rep came into being. Suffice it to say that it was a commercial enterprise operating in an area of then considerable affluence.

Fortunately my request for 'memories' in the Manchester Evening News brought me letters from people who remembered it well and were regular visitors; plus some who performed there, including Dame Wendy Hiller, who is, happily, still with us.

It is, perhaps, significant that, throughout its seventeen years existence, the Manchester Guardian sent a drama critic to review the plays presented on a weekly change basis. It, therefore, seems fair to assume, on this evidence, that the standard of productions, and the choice of plays, was not so poor, otherwise the Manchester Guardian would not have bothered.

Thanks to microfilming one can now 'whizz' through the pages of the Manchester Guardian and read, at random, the Tuesday evaluations. One rarely finds any comment to the effect that "this being Weekly Rep one could not expect any better". On the contrary the acting is constantly remarked upon as being good and some times of a high order.

Further evidence that the theatre was supported by the professional personnel of Manchester is to be seen in the lists of the names of the people who subscribed to the Lea Axon Guarantee Scheme. The programme note states that "A guarantee consists of indemnifying the Theatre against loss to the extent of £10 spread over the next FIVE YEARS, not more than £2 to be called up in any one year." There are approximately 450 names and of these 30 are doctors, either of medicine, or another subject.

I am grateful to James Smith, now in his seventies, for the following account of this Repertory Co. He was a student at the old Manchester School of Art and spent his life designing wrought ironwork, tiling, and electrical control and switchgear.

He writes, "Your letter in the Evening News revived memories of regular playgoing at the Rusholme Repertory theatre which gave me a first taste of drama at a price a young man could just about afford.

That time was in the middle twenties and thirties and I paid 1/6d for a good seat every Saturday night. The theatre had been a garage or stable for the Liverpool Carriage Co., and it had a great advantage in that you could see the stage from every seat, a feature not considered essential by many architects (or managements for that matter!). The acoustics were very good. There was no gallery if I remember correctly. At one time there was no licensed bar and patrons used a pub across Wilmslow Road where a bell was rung when the interval was ending. A new play was presented each week, and how the company played and rehearsed was a mystery only known to the producer, the actor manager (and the actors!). The clientele was a regular one and there was always a good 'house'.

The clientele at Rusholme Rep was mixed socially. No doubt the type of play varied the social mixture in the audiences, but generally the bias was what for want of a better name is known as middle class. I suppose there were reasons for this bias, in that Rusholme and Fallowfield were areas whose residents were associated with Owen's college as teachers and lecturers, and also, even in those days, there was a considerable foreign population of professional people and shopkeepers who came from Europe generally, where theatre played a strong role in intellectual life.

Nearby, Victoria Park was then a private estate with a population of successful bankers, merchants, and professional people and no doubt this contributed towards the audiences at the theatre. A similar class of audience was drawn from East Didsbury. To fix these people politically I should say they were liberals, or liberal minded, and read the then Manchester Guardian.

Among the plays I saw was 'Draw the Fires' by Ernst Toller with a theme of revolt in the German navy towards the end of the first World War. 'Draw the Fires' must have been special because the play was on sale in the foyer for 2/6d. The production must have taxed the company and the scene builders considerably because the play requires a cast of forty-one and eleven entirely different scenes."

Nancy Poultney, who later became a director, started her theatrical life at Rusholme. She wrote, "My first Weekly Rep experience as a young actress was with the Rusholme Rep. It was remarkable for many reasons. An old tram shed turned into a theatre with many drawbacks, but it had a high reputation in the profession and I remember how thrilled I was to get into the company – that was in the very early thirties. The producer was a man called Clifford Marks, I don't remember how good a producer he was but I do know he was a good chooser of people. One he had chosen was to go on to play in films, plays, and TV. Her name? ....Wendy Hiller!"

Dame Wendy Hiller commented on those early days of a distinguished career, "I have very happy memories of Manchester Repertory Theatre (at Rusholme) and wish there were more theatres like it for the young actors and actresses today."[4]

---

[1] 'Neville Cardus', Autobiography, William Collins, Sons and Company Ltd. [1947].
[2] As above.
[3] 'The Selective Ego', Ed. Tim Beaumont, Harrap Ltd. [1976].
[4] Letter to author.

Chapter 7

Bristol Little Theatre [1923-49]

In the year 1923 that saw the revival of Repertory in a Manchester suburb, further south, in Bristol, a group of theatre enthusiasts were meeting to try and establish a Repertory company.

As is so often the case in pioneering work, though many may express interest in the project, the man who undertook the organisation and secretarial work was a Mr. Stanley Hill, then Hon. Secretary of the Bristol Rotary Club.

The Colston Hall was hired and on the advice of St. John Ervine, Mr. Rupert Harvey, of the Old Vic, was engaged to form a company and direct the plays.

In the course of my research the name of St. John Ervine appeared again and again, and he seemed to embody the essence of friendship as we find it expressed by the writer of the Book of Proverbs "A friend loveth at all times" and, more significantly – "Faithful are the wounds of a friend".

Again and again one finds him criticising this and that Repertory company for what he regarded as weaknesses, but this would always be accompanied by words of encouragement. Head and heart were well balanced. He recognised that the final judgement of a play was in seeing it played, and not as a mere literary work to be contemplated by well meaning academics in the study, or lecture room, only.

In a publication recording the work of the first two seasons at the Bristol Little Theatre, for which he wrote an introduction, he states "This Little Theatre is not the theatre of a clique: it is the theatre of a community. It takes all sorts to make a world, and a wise manager bears that fact prominently in his mind. There is an austerely-minded person who would have your playgoers all of a kind, insisting that only the more difficult works of the masters shall be performed in repertory theatres. Hamlet, yes, but Twelfth Night, no! The austerely-minded person seldom puts any of his money into the enterprises he so ardently desires. Some very austerely-minded persons are even reluctant to pay for their seats at the plays they advocate on the plea that they are entitled to free accommodation because of their interest in the higher drama. I suffered for eight months from such persons when, for my sins, I managed the Abbey Theatre in Dublin. Those who are responsible for Bristol's Little Theatre have wisely ignored the austerely-minded person and have resolved that their theatre shall be one where all intelligent persons shall find intelligent recreation, rather than a place where melancholy men, and misunderstood women, may twiddle their souls." [1]

The subsequent development of this Little theatre was typical of so many of the repertories. There were good and bad times – occasionally they would find themselves on the brink of closure only to be saved by a generous donation from a well wisher, or a revival of interest when it was made known that the theatre would have to close unless more support was forthcoming.

The success of the Repertories was due to talented players working together as a team, but this was often achieved by

Illustration 7.1 Colston Hall: Bristol Little Theatre

inspired production and, in 1935, Ronald Russell returned to the Bristol Little Theatre as the Producer.

He first joined the company in 1929.

"A Bristolian born and bred, and direct from Clifton College which he left on a day and started his Studentship at the Theatre on the next. Chaffed by his colleagues as suffering from what they called "a Clifton accent", his principal work at first was to light the gas heater and deliver hot water to the dressing rooms, graduating during his two-and-a-half years' stay to the position of Assistant Stage Manager."

Under his direction the theatre survived and, aided by Grizell Kinross, who gave financial aid until the company was able to maintain itself, continued to provide a 'mixed bag' of entertaining plays.

It should be noted that here, as with other Repertories, during the war from 1939-45, the task of managing the company fell to two very capable women; in this instance Peggy Ann Wood, Ronald Russell's wife, as producer, and Evelyn F. Osborne as manager. (At the Theatre Royal, Windsor, this task was undertaken by the wife of John Counsell).

Ronald Russell states "From 1929-49, apart from a year's touring, I directed and/or stage-managed or acted in Weekly Rep and have never had cause to regret it."

He remarks, "The great problem with Weekly Rep lay in the casting. One carried a permanent company, making a few changes in the break between seasons, for at least 40 to 50 weeks. If you were able to secure the rights of plays which were suitable for the company you had, in other words your casting was right, it was possible to achieve a very high standard indeed. But when you decided to put on a play, where there was inevitably going to be one or more pieces of unsuitable casting, miscasting in fact, then your standard began to decline.

On the other hand, between 1915 and say 1950, you were not in the era of TV and so many good and highly experienced actors were free and willing to work in Weekly Rep (especially if they were bringing up a family and with the prospect of a long season or sometimes series of seasons). Ralph Hutton, for example, spent 11 years under the old B.L.T. management, and then came back and worked for me from 1936 till his death in 1944, and I remember him as a very fine actor indeed.

Another reason why Weekly Rep was good was because it

meant 'teamwork'. A regular resident company learnt to rely on one another especially if, as was our policy, leading parts were shared and if you played 'Hamlet' this week, you could hope to play the manservant 'Lane' in 'The Importance' next week. It also made promising actors into good actors more quickly by

Illustration 7.2 Ralph Hutton – Bristol Little Theatre
"We had a wonderful senior member of the company – a fine actor. One Ralph Hutton". Sir Michael Hordern.

stretching them. I feel certain Michael Hordern, Cyril Luck-ham, Lockwood West, Peggy Thorpe Bates, who all worked for me at the start of their careers, would tell you the same.

I would not wish us to go back to Weekly Rep, indeed at the third attempt the Rapier Players converted to fortnightly pro-ductions and so continued from 1949-1963. But I regret the fact that today so many Repertory companies, especially those nearer to London, cast each play from scratch and that teamwork and camaraderie of a close knit bond of players is often lost."

Mervyn Johns, whom cinema enthusiasts will remember (some of which now appear on TV) was with the company for seven years, playing a great variety of parts; and it is of interest to note that his daughter Glynis made her first stage appear-ance here during the time her father was a member of the company.

Illustration 7.3 Lockwood West and Michael Hordern in 'Alf's Button' – Bristol Little Theatre, 1937

Illustration 7.4 Three Sisters by Chekhov – Bristol Little Theatre Production

Sir Michael Hordern, C.B.E. commented further on his experience at Bristol and more generally on Weekly Rep. He wrote "When I am interviewed about my CV I never fail to say that Ronald Russell turned me into a "pro". His was a marvellous discipline. He knew to a half-hour how much direction he could give in the week at his disposal. "Take two minutes a page before your first entrance" was your rehearsal call for the next morning and woe betide you if you were late. I was at Bristol for two successive seasons of 45 weeks each! A week out every couple of months or so. Reps certainly deserve better than the "cursory dismissal" that you mention, and there's another side to the equation that tends to be forgotten – the audiences. From Hastings and Plymouth to Dundee the theatres were not "cursorily dismissed" by the inhabitants. It was weekly rep that kept drama, theatre, alive and the population over all, more aware of the live stage than it is today; even the advent of the cinema didn't kill it. I suppose TV is the culprit. The main thing is that it taught us, or began to teach us, our jobs and there are little disciplines from those far off days that keep coming back to me. As I turn out the lights in No. 1 dressing room at the NT or the Old Vic (Sir Michael Hordern on the door) I always remember Ronald Russell telling us "Switching off the dressing room lights might make just the difference between profit and loss on the week"."[2]

---

[1] 'A Short History of Bristol's Little Theatre', First and Second Seasons, [1923-24-25], Bristol, Partridge & Love, [1925].
[2] Letter to author

Chapter 8

Coventry
[1931-40]

Of the many Weekly Repertories that existed throughout the country before the Second World War, the one that performed at the old Opera House, in Coventry, was greatly appreciated by the theatregoers of that city, until its destruction, by bombing, in 1940.

One cannot always prove that there is a necessary link between one event and a later one, but it is significant that Coventry was the first city to build a new theatre – the Belgrade [1958] – after the war; and this could be partly attributed to the enthusiasm of those theatregoers who, having lost their repertory theatre, wished to revive repertory in Coventry.

The response to my request for 'memories and impressions' in the local paper included a scrap-book that Mabel Baxendale had made. One of the saddest things for a researcher to hear, or read, must be – "I had photographs, and a scrap-book of newspaper cuttings about the theatre, but I threw them all away when we moved house"; or – "they were all destroyed when the house was bombed during the war".

Turning the pages one sees the youthful features of Ann Casson (daughter of Lewis Casson and Sybil Thorndike). A correspondent wrote "At the time 'The Distaff Side' was offered Ann Casson, daughter of Sybil Thorndike, was a member of the repertory, and we were greatly honoured by the role of the Matriarch being taken superbly by Sybil herself. I am sure her presence brought the best out of all the cast for it made a lasting impression and proved, too, that a superfluity of women in no way detracted from the appeal of a play."

Phylis Calvert played there. She is better known as a filmstar, one of her most memorable performances being that of the mother of the deaf child in 'Mandy'. There is the young Pauline Letts, who later married one of the producers there, namely Geoffrey Staines, who later worked at the York Repertory. Alec

McCowen, says of him in his autobiographical book 'Young Gemini' "But eventually an agent called Nora Nelson King befriended me. She got me an interview with Geoffrey Staines, the director of a fine company at the Theatre Royal, York. I managed to curb my tongue and he engaged me as Assistant Stage Manager and to play small parts. This was my home for the next eighteen months. My father called me 'the York Ham'. I was given parts to play and learnt a great deal from Geoffrey Staines' direction. The weeks sped by and I could walk the mile from the digs to the theatre without once raising my head from the current script. I think this must have been when I memorised my lines because according to my diaries I saw at least two films a week and read at least two books."

The scrap-book contains a photograph of the Repertory Circle's members attending the annual dance. The significant thing is that some are wearing evening dress which seemed to indicate a predominantly middle-class clientele, a point which I raised with Mabel Baxendale. Her reply was interesting. "Your query about the type of audience – it was completely across the

Illustration 8.1 Coventry Rep. [1931-40] Repertory Circle's Annual Dance

class structure. I am of working class parents and so are many of my friends – my father was a tool maker who served his seven years apprenticeship in Crewe works and then was thrown out when he completed it and eventually found work in Coventry. I never aspired to the annual Repertory dance but I'm sure it would be a very mixed gathering. Pre-war a dance meant a long dress or skirt, after the depravation of the Great Strike I think we were all aiming for something better. The pre-war Coventrians (and pre TV) were quite avid theatregoers for both the Repertory and the Hippodrome with its variety – perhaps that was why the Belgrade theatre was built so soon after the war and the older 'city fathers' are keen to support it."

That the Repertories were regarded as offering, on occasions, a more serious kind of entertainment is amusingly illustrated in the following extract from another Coventry correspondent – "A friend who boarded a tram in Broadgate passed the Opera and 'Hippo' just as people were leaving; she said she wouldn't go to the Opera because when she passed there the people who were coming out were so solemn faced, while those emerging from the 'Hippo' were always laughing."

Janet Burnell who played there as the leading lady in the 1935/36 seasons, before leaving to play in the West End, writes "I was at Coventry September 35/36 and was released from my contract May 11th 1936 for a lead in a West End production. This was a lovely real theatre. Good dressing-rooms on three floors, mine was stage level with wash basin, plenty of room for one's dress basket and a comfortable armchair. There was room for quick changes on the stage unlike Croydon. A lovely dresser, "Mabel", (no dressers or help at Croydon). Mabel would produce hot tea and coffee and go to the bars for drinks and out for sandwiches or snacks even. Old, and plump, and puffing, but always cheerful, and helpful, and willing, a wonderful person – the "salt", of the theatre."

Many of the plays performed by the Weekly Repertory companies were West End comedy successes and the Playgoers Circle organised trips to London.

At least two special trains ran from Coventry to the West End so that the fans could see West End productions – apparently with the idea of comparing them – unfavourably of course – with the productions they had seen in Coventry.

Perhaps the last word – though by no means the final one – on this Midland Weekly Repertory should be that of Mabel Baxendale – "To talk with older Coventrians on buses, and many still live in the old districts, very often the conversation comes round to the days of the 'Rep', and when I re-read the list of plays in the scrap-book, I thought some of those are still around too!"

Chapter 9

Birmingham (Alexandra)
[1927-43]
and
Wolverhampton (Grand)
[1936-66]

Not far from the old Birmingham Repertory Theatre there is the Alexandra Theatre. This theatre was bought by Leon Salberg in 1911, whose sons, Derek and Reggie, proved to be as success-ful as their father in balancing good commercial sense with astute discernment of the taste of different sections of the public.

Unless you are receiving money from public funds, and not entirely dependent on the box office takings, you need to develop a sensitive antenna to gauge what potential theatre-goers will pay to see.

There is considerable evidence to show that Leon Salberg, and subsequently his son Derek, served the theatre-goers of Bir-mingham with theatrical entertainment of a high order. Enter-tainment that included an annual pantomime which saw almost every leading variety artist, from Barry Lupino to Les Dawson, appearing at the 'Alex'.

The Alexandra theatre has been the venue for such diverse talents as those possessed by the famous duo Morecambe & Wise, Laurence Olivier, and Marlene Dietrich.

On the occasion of Derek Salberg's retirement one of the many tributes paid to him and the Alex was by J. C. Trewin. He wrote, "It was always a genuine pleasure to go to the Alexandra. Some theatres are immediately welcoming, some, emphatically, are not... My predecessor, Tom Kemp, used to say that the Alex under Derek Salberg – following family tradition – was a theatre that, with Barrie's Island, liked to be visited. He was right. You did feel in the atmosphere of the Alex that play going was an event... Such a house as the Alexandra is respected far beyond any regional limit."

The Repertory companies were employed after the pantomime had finished – usually running for about 12 weeks.

Leon's first venture into Repertory came about on 28th March, 1927 when the first Repertory company was launched at the Alexandra Theatre. This almost corresponded with the opening of the Northampton Repertory theatre on 10th January, 1927.

The early days of Repertory at the Alexandra, as described by M. K. Fraser in his book published in 1948, are interesting as they again recall the difficulties faced by the pioneers of Repertory who could not afford to lose a lot of money. He writes, "In the beginning it was a twice-nightly, play-a-week system, maintained by a company of some dozen or fifteen resident players, who were enough to cast the majority of the plays chosen, and who, when an extra large cast was required, were

Illustration 9.1 Leon Salberg (Alexandra Theatre, Birmingham)

reinforced by local amateurs and semi-amateurs from the dramatic societies, the stage schools and so on."

After detailing some of the inadequacies of twice-nightly, weekly change performances at the Alex in these early days, Fraser continues, "A dog's life? Oh, yes. A slave's existence? Certainly. Everybody miserable? Everybody bearing a load of mischief on his back, a burden of depression in her mien? Oh no. Certainly not. The wonder of it was that there was never any difficulty in recruiting a reasonably sound company for twice-nightly, weekly "rep" and that, with a few exceptions, those recruited seemed to enjoy the slavery and thrive on the drudgery.

They found time to sleep, and eat, and shop, and pay calls, and go out to the hospitable homes and clubs thrown open to them. They went to other theatres' matinees, and thought how lucky they were not to have to play in the afternoon. The Leading Man

Illustration 9.2 Derek Salberg, C.B.E., O.St.J., J.P.

(less frequently the Leading Lady) opened bazaars, addressed Rotary clubs, wrote articles for the house magazine. On Saturday nights (when they should have gone straight home to start a good long night's slumber) they all trooped up to the office (the "Alec" Saturday night "offices" are famous throughout the business), drank the Guv'nor's drinks, and talked shop until, any time in the small hours, even the most thirsty and/or the most loquacious decided it was time to call it a day.

How was it done? How was it done? One can best answer that question by reference to the inexhaustible vivacity and vitality of the profession, and to the incontrovertible truth that you can get used to anything. Besides, there is well-known to be a special Providence looking after drunkards and children – and the stage is largely peopled by children of mature years."

During the second World War the BBC news was being read when the building was hit by a bomb and the explosion heard by all of the listeners. The newsreader's name was Bruce Belfrage.

That he kept 'his cool' and went on reading the news may have owed something to his year as leading man at the Alexandra theatre in 1928.

In his autobiography 'One Man in His Time' (1951) he comments on the advantages of being a versatile actor stating that this ability had proved a godsend to him in television. He writes, "such ability as I possess in this respect was acquired entirely in Repertory and chiefly at the Alexandra Theatre, Birmingham. As leading man in 1928 at this theatre, I played forty entirely different leading parts in forty weeks twice nightly. An exhausting experience, but one which has provided me with a firm foundation on which to build up a study of any character I may be asked to create.

The policy of Leon Salberg, father of the present manager, was to find a leading man and a leading lady – frequently, as in my case, totally unknown – pay them really good salaries and plaster the town with their names so that they became in a very short time household words to every citizen of Birmingham. Every week the same customers sat in the same seats at the same performance; many of them wrote, came round to call after the show or offered hospitality in their homes. I made a number of good friends, and have kept them.

It was really hard work, particularly as I had to follow Henry

Hallatt, who was leading man during the previous year. He had been immensely popular and the audiences at the start of the season were inclined to be shy of anyone who had replaced their favourite.

Leon Salberg expected to get what he was paying for. He knew very well that he would only get the best out of a contented company and he saw to it that he had one. The pay was good, the dressing-rooms clean and comfortable, and after the last house on Saturday nights he always entertained us all to drinks and sandwiches in his office.

"Here," he said, "you will find me, my producer and my business manager. If you have troubles, speak. Do not mutter to yourselves or complain one to the other!" The result was that the atmosphere of harmony, without which such a job would have been impossible, existed in full measure.

Here was a truly remarkable man. His vocabulary was somewhat limited; it was sometimes a little confusing when he persistently alluded to everything from a play to a piano as the "Vot you call it down dere" – but he was a shrewd, kindly, agreeable person for whom I shall always retain the greatest admiration and affection."

The Repertory company at the 'Alex' had been run in the manner of the old stock companies where actors were engaged to play leading roles, or character, juvenile, etc., parts.

This sometimes led to unfortunate results – the particular actor, perhaps, not being physically suited for a particular part!

So, the 1934 repertory season was to be different. Still twice-nightly, but everyone was to play as cast; no longer was there to be a leading man and a leading lady.

Writing of that year, more than forty years later, Derek Salberg states, "That year the plays included Elmer Rice's "Street Scene", Shaw's "Candida", Besier's "Barrets of Wimpole Street" and James Bridie's "Sleeping Clergyman", all of which, unfortunately, had to be cut owing to the exigencies of the twice-nightly system, but it must be stressed that, and I know most young actors of today would not easily believe this, standards, although variable, were, for the most part, very high." [1]

There are few men, who have been associated with the theatre of this century, better placed than Derek Salberg to make such a judgement.

In 1938, after the death of his father, he became England's

youngest theatre manager and, with the exception of the war years, continued to run the Alex successfully until his retirement in July 1977.

In 1943, when the air raids were infrequent, and no competition as yet from TV, the Repertory became a fortnightly one, and remained such until 1975.

In 1936 Leon Salberg, having met P. J. Purdey, the general manager at the Grand Theatre, Wolverhampton when business was not so good, offered to put in a Repertory company for a trial period of four weeks. The trial period was extended to twenty weeks and this was to continue until 1966 when repertory finished. Derek Salberg introduced pantomime to the Grand; but apart from this the remainder of the year was taken up with Weekly Rep.

I have already quoted Peggy Mount on her experience at Wolverhampton. The devotion and pride in 'their Rep' so often displayed in letters from regular Rep attenders is evident in the following. "What a pity when Peggy Mount found fame in the West End and on TV – she was only given comedy roles. That is where rep scores, it uses all the talents of the players to the full. The Derek Salberg Repertory company was a truly first rate one, some of my happiest hours were spent watching them."

So – the price of fame!

The following was sent to me by David Manderson, who was the manager of the Grand Theatre, Wolverhampton, before Mr. Purdey occupied that position.

Extract from a letter to myself from David Manderson ... "The enclosed photostat is the one event that startled me. It was after I had left Wolverhampton and was acting as London Rep. for the Salbergs. Need I say we never took advantage of Shaw's suggestion. I met his secretary some years later and she well remembered how amused the 'Master' had been by the incident."

Birmingham (Alexandra) and Wolverhampton (Grand)

Wolverhampton Repertory Company - 1951

Illustration 9.3 Wolverhampton Repertory Company – 1951

Illustration 9.4 Gerald Cuff. "One of the best actors with whom I ever worked and from whom I learnt so much." – Kenneth More.

4, Whitehall Court,
London, S.W.1.

2nd December 1938.

My licence for the performance of my play *Pygmalion* by the Derek Salberg Company in Wolverhampton did not include an authorisation to advertise it as "the brilliant comedy by Oscar Wilde".

Is Oscar's name a bigger draw than mine? and if so what royalty do his representatives receive for its use?

G. Bernard Shaw

The reply to Shaw was as follows:

Dear Sir - I regret that some confusion in the mind of the resident manager of the Grand Theatre, Wolverhampton, caused him last week to attribute to the late Mr. Wilde a play which, I understand, was written by you.

Mr. Purdey, (the gentleman in question) is disinclined to offer an apology as he contends that this substitution accounts for the show having played to approximately three times as much money as it did when he billed it as being written by you. He also contends that this will result in your receiving larger royalties than he believes would otherwise have been the case and he is therefore unable to see what you are grumbling about.

Shaw's reply on a signed postcard was:

"Please give my compliments to Mr. Purdey; and beg him to continue the attribution, which was a most happy thought. I am not grumbling; I am rejoicing."

G. Bernard Shaw

---

[1] 'My Love Affair with a Theatre', [1978].

Chapter 10

York
[1935-64]

Weekly Rep in York began, on an all the year round basis, in 1935, but before that there was seasonal Weekly Rep run by Percy Hutchinson.

The impact of this company was sufficiant enough to move the playwright John Galsworthy to write to Hutchinson claiming "Enterprises like this repertory theatre in York afford the best means of keeping life blood flowing in the body of the British drama." Percy Hutchinson went bankrupt before he could form a permanent company for the Theatre Royal; and in 1934 the lease of the Theatre Royal was taken over by a group of small shareholders who raised a capital of £2,300 in £1 shares and formed the York citizens' Theatre Limited (later to become a Trust).

E. Martin Browne was the first producer and the company lost money. The directors looked elsewhere for a producer and Redvers B. Leech who had been running a sucoessful company at Coventry, was engaged. Sybil Rosenfeld, who has chronicled the history of the Theatre Royal up to 1948, writes of this period, "It was largely due to his efforts that the York Citizens' Theatre turned the corner to success. The new regime instituted twice nightly performances at 6.30 and 8.50 and a drastic reduction of prices which enabled the Theatre to compete with the cinemas. The old and new charges were as follows:

		Old	*New*
93	dress circle first two rows	3/6d	2/6d
145	dress circle remainder	3/6d	1/6d
361	stalls	3/6d	1/6d
123	pit	1/6d	9d
268	upper circle	1/6d	7d
260	gallery	9d	4d
1250			

The result was that almost from the start attendances rose to 10,000 a week. A system of block booking by which twelve tickets could be purchased at a further reduction was also introduced."[1]

These early days saw the further development of two outstanding players who are still active, namely Pauline Letts and Phyllis Calvert. Redvers Leech's move from Coventry (where they were both working) may have had something to do with their arrival in York; and over the years the Weekly Rep companies here saw the emergence of some well known players, but, as indicated in Chapter 1, this would be no more than 5% of the total number who played there and gave weekly pleasure to thousands of the citizens of York.

Geoffrey Staines, who was also a producer at Coventry, moved to York in 1941 and successfully steered the company through the war years and beyond.

He eventually gave way to Donald Bodley, who had a long and productive association with the theatre. Norman Hoult, who had gained valuable experience at the Bristol Little Theatre under the direction of Ronald Russell, joined the company as an actor and later as a producer.

From the opening in 1935 to 1941 this company operated, as did the majority of Weekly Reps, on a twice nightly basis, a precedent which, to present day actors, must seem to have been an exhausting prospect. Accepting the fact that to cover expenses playing twice nightly was a necessity, some of the actors welcomed it!

With relatively little time for rehearsing each play, the extra performances, with an audience, were also extra playing times, so that by Wednesday evening they had been through the play six times – plus the dress rehearsal, and with an audience. Phyllis Calvert wrote, "I spent three years in 'Rep'. One year with Roy Limbert's Malvern Co., one year at Coventry, and a year at York. I played every age from 12 years to old ladies and at York played 26 leading parts in as many weeks, twice nightly. I do not know how young people nowadays ever get practical experience which was so very valuable to me. I enjoyed every moment."[2]

Amongst others, now well known, who worked at York during the years of Weekly Rep, we find Jean Alexander, Hilda Ogden of 'Coronation Street'; Bernard Hepton, Pauline Yates, John

Alderton and Pauline Letts.

In her book 'The Other Side of the Street', Jean Alexander speaks of "the slavery of Weekly Rep". It is a necessary condition of being a slave that one cannot escape from that condition. At any time during the years she was working in Weekly Rep I'm sure that she could have returned to a job in a library, the work she was doing before joining the Adelphi Guild Players; the company I was with for four years. Perhaps that seemed a more slavish prospect! I remember her as a quiet, undemonstrative, actress; far removed from any popular conception of a 'showbiz personality'. She was transformed by her playing of another role on stage. She was also further proof that one could spend many years in Weekly Rep and remain a fine actress. She states "I perfected my craft in Weekly Rep."

---

[1] 'The York Theatre', Sybil Rosenfeld [1948].
[2] Letter to author.

York Theatre Admission Prices

Year	Dress Circle (Reserved)	Circle (Reserved)	Orch. Stalls (Reserved)	Upper Pit	Circle	Gallery
1935	2s 6d	1s 6d	1s 6d	9d	7d	4d
1945	3s 6d	2s 6d	2s 6d	1s 3d	1s 0d	6d
1955	4s 3d	3s 3d	1s 9d	1s 9d	1s 6d	1s 0d
1965	9s 0d		8s 6d	6s 0d	5s 6d	2s 6d
			7s 6d			
1975	£1.40		£1.10			
			£0.85			
1985	£4.75		£2.75			
			£4.00			

Chapter 11

Edinburgh, Royal Lyceum [1940-55]

There were Weekly Reps in Scotland, mainly in Dundee, Perth and Edinburgh; and the one I now wish to consider is that of the Wilson Barrett Co., which performed at the Lyceum theatre, Edinburgh, between 1940 and 1955.

This was not on the basis of a forty-five week run of weekly change, as was the case with most Weekly Reps, but the year would begin with an average fifteen week run at the Lyceum, then move to the Glasgow Alhambra, where they would stay for the summer, returning to the Lyceum from September until Christmas.

Wilson Barrett was the grandson of the well known Victorian actor-manager of the same name. His Scottish connection began with his joining another company playing on a weekly change basis, namely, the Jevan Brandon-Thomas repertory company.

This company played their first season at the Lyceum in 1930. This was only of a six week duration when they returned south, playing a number of successful seasons in Bournemouth.

In 1933 they were asked to return to the Lyceum by Andrew Cruikshank, the manager for Howard and Wyndam Limited. This was to mark the beginning of Repertory activity which, for the greater part of the time was on a weekly change basis and was to continue for two decades.

I remarked earlier that theatrical enterprises have often owed their success to the vision, combined with 'both feet on the ground' awareness of existing realities, of remarkable individuals, who were prepared to work hard themselves and inspire others to do likewise.

The use of the word 'commercial' to denote some kind of inferior activity due to the soiling of one's hands in handling money obtained by offering some pleasure, and even uplift, to people who, of their own free choice, have paid for this – is nowhere more given 'the lie' than in the work of Jevan Brandon-Thomas and Wilson Barrett. The latter, fortunately, left us a record, and comment, of his companies' activities in Edinburgh and Glasgow in a book entitled 'On Stage for Notes' (1954).

Dare anyone even suggest that the subsidy now offered to many theatrical companies is always honestly employed? That there is never over-manning of staff; no purchasing of equipment in excess of requirement?

How many of the 'non-commercial' companies could exist without having some 'commerce' with the rest of the tainted world?

I have pointed out (Chapter 1) that only a very small percentage of all of the repertories thousands of actors and actresses became 'stars', or well known. Brandon-Thomas and Wilson Barrett gathered together a remarkable team of actors and actresses who built up a reputation for fine acting which

Illustration 11.1 Wilson Barrett (Edinburgh Royal Lyceum, 1940-55)

attracted a consistent support from the citizens of Edinburgh and Glasgow. These came from all walks of life.

Donald Campbell, who has fairly chronicled the history of the Royal Lyceum in his book 'A Brighter Sunshine' (1983) says of the Brandon-Thomas company, "During the course of 1935, for instance, the company produced no fewer than thirty-one plays by a wide variety of authors, including Barrie, Coward, Maugham, Priestley, Arnold Bennett, John Drinkwater, Frederick Lonsdale, Arnold Ridley and Harold Brighouse. In addition to those, there were several new plays, often by Scottish authors like Donald Carswell, Robins Millar, William Templeton and Elizabeth Drew. Since each play would receive no more than a week's rehearsal, followed by a week's performance, an actor would generally have three parts on his hands at any point in the season – the part he was playing, the part he was rehearsing and the part he was about to rehearse.

Jevan Brandon-Thomas's personal contribution to the season was enormous. Actor, director, playwright and business manager, he also found time to handle the company's public relations, writing a great number of articles about the company for any publication which was prepared to print them."

It was during the Brandon-Thomas company's occupation of the Lyceum stage that the most successful production seen there this century took place.

This was not the production of a classic, but of a new play written by an actress named Margot Lister. It is based on the life of Mary, Queen of Scots, and entitled 'Swords about the Cross'.

Donald Campbell records, "This was an ambitious, hugely expensive production, employing a cast of thirty-three actors, plus an equivalent number of supers, with incidental music played by the internationally renowned Elizabethan ensemble, the Dolmetsch Orchestra.

The part of Mary was played by a pretty young actress called Nancy Hornsby, Darnley by Wilson Barrett, and Bothwell by Jevan Brandon-Thomas himself, standing in for Owen Reynolds, who had taken ill at the last moment. Well down the cast, in the tiny part of Kirkcaldy of Grange, was a young Scottish actor, James Donald, who would later, despite illness, make a substantial career in films. Unlike most Brandon-Thomas productions, 'Swords about the Cross' ran for two weeks rather than one, but that tells only half the story. The demand for tickets was so great that four extra matinees had to be added in the first week – on Tuesday, Wednesday, Thursday and Friday – making eighteen performances in all. Taking every performance into account, the play was seen by 42,000 people, a figure which assumes even greater significance when one realises that the previous year (1935) the management had instituted alterations to the building which had reduced the capacity from 2,500 to 1,650. Somehow or other, an extra 650 people were accommodated in the theatre every night and the play achieved the amazing percentage of 125 per cent of capacity for the run of the play.

Press coverage of the play was extensive and Swords About the Cross made a small piece of broadcasting history. On the opening night, 25th May 1936, Robin Stark gave an eye-witness impression of the event for the Scottish Home Service – the first time that this had ever been done in Scotland."

Life, not just theatrical life, is in the main unpredictable; not only in the sense of unpleasant, and sometimes tragic happenings occurring when all seemed set for a pleasant journey; but also in the sense of pleasant surprises when all seemed 'doom and gloom'.

The Brandon-Thomas company seemed set fair for a long stay at the Lyceum when Andrew Cruikshank and Brandon-Thomas quarrelled. The cause of this disagreement is not known and, since the persons concerned are now dead, it will remain a matter of speculation.

Brandon-Thomas had built up a fine team of players who became very popular with the Edinburgh audiences. There were no 'stars', and he said that all of his players were leading actors; but some were more popular than others and these included Wilson Barrett.

In the Sunday Times of 9th March, 1941, there appeared a review by James Agate of a production of J. B. Priestley's 'When We Are Married'. Remembering that Agate was the leading drama critic at that time and, consequently, familiar with the acting currently occurring on the London stage, his opening remarks seem significant. He wrote, "The remarkable thing about repertory companies is the excellence of their acting". He then recalls his early days, reviewing for the Manchester Guardian the productions at the Gaiety. He remarked, "The three wives are beautifully played by Miss Kitty de Legh, Miss Sybil Wise and Miss Ellen Compton."

Those names would be familiar to Edinburgh audiences as members of the Brandon-Thomas company, but here they were playing together under the direction of Wilson Barrett; the beginning of an adventurous association that, for some, was to continue until 1955.

It was typical of Wilson Barrett's courage and determination that whilst on 5th March, 1940, he was involved in a serious railway accident, and his spine was crushed and his pelvis fractured in two places, he continued to manage the company from his hospital bed.

The Scottish connection began on 27th May, 1941, when they opened at the Alhambra theatre, Glasgow; producing a play, on a weekly change basis, for fifteen weeks. They were invited to follow this with a six week season at the Royal Lyceum Theatre, Edinburgh; and this was so successful that they were asked to stay on until Christmas.

All of these plays were produced by Charles Hickman. The majority of the plays, during its fifteen year run at the Lyceum, were produced by either Barrett himself or Richard Mathews, Clare Harris, Joan Kemp-Welch and C. B. Pulman.

Bearing in mind that the initial years were the war years, plus his unfortunate accident, with all, the restrictions imposed by the shortage of male actors, and the scarcity of materials; Wilson Barrett managed to do the seemingly impossible in putting on plays at all.

In 1943, when he was almost at his wits end in finding a solution to the producer shortage, when all seemed 'doom and gloom' the unpredictable happened. In Wilson's own words "I think it was only about three weeks before we were due to open that Nuna Davey, who had been one of my hopes until I heard that she was definitely going into a new play by Emlyn Williams, rang me up from London and asked me if I had ever thought of Clare Harris.

Up to that time my only knowledge of Clare Harris was that she was a very fine actress whose work I had often seen and always admired. One of the things I shall never forget is the first night of a production of 'Much Ado About Nothing' at the New Theatre in London, with Henry Ainley as Benedict, Madge Titheradge as Beatric, Clare Harris as Hero."

Of their first meeting he wrote, "Her charm, her beauty, and above all that thing which was so particularly Clare, a mixture I think of sound common-sense and real love for, and interest in, humanity, had conquered me completely. I could not know then, of course, all that she was going to mean to us for the next six years, but I did see quite plainly that if her production work matched her personality, then at all costs I must try to keep her with us. Fortunately this did not prove very difficult.

Our first play this season was 'Spring Tide' by J. B. Priestley and George Billam, and the rehearsal week remains in my memory as one of the happiest I have ever spent. After the horrors of the past year, Clare's cool, calm production methods, her bubbling sense of fun, her faculty for getting right down to the heart of a character and giving you in one sentence just the thing you wanted to know, and above all her unfailing intuition on what was right and what was wrong in a production, came as the most blessed relief."

She was to stay for six years, producing many plays on a weekly change basis, though not, as with some Weekly Reps ever doing forty-five plays, or more, in a year. In 1943 she produced nine of the thirteen plays put on at the Lyceum between 16th February and 15th May, six of the thirteen plays at the Alhambra Glasgow, between 24th May and 21st August; and then five of the plays when the company returned to Edinburgh from 14th September to 18th December.

Some of the plays produced in Edinburgh in the spring were played later in Glasgow, and some of the Glasgow new productions were played again during the autumn season in Edinburgh.

It was during her first year as a producer that the company played 'Romeo and Juliet'. As I have indicated, designing and building a set during the war was a difficult business and the balcony scene presented a particular problem. Help came from an unexpected source. W. Barrett records, "About a month before our production was due, John Gielgud was in Edinburgh playing in 'Love for Love', and he and Clare being old friends, she gave a supper party for him in her rooms one night after the show, during which we happened to mention our difficulties. We didn't leave Clare's that night until after one o'clock, but by eleven the next morning Gielgud was in the Lyceum. During our morning break for coffee he gave Clare a design for a standing setting (which he said was a combination of an early production of his at Oxford, when he used the bare Elizabethan stage, and of his recent elaborately built production at the New Theatre in London) and a sheaf of notes indicating where each scene could be played. I can't think that he had had time to sleep at all that night, but the result was brilliant. We could have played the whole play without ever dropping the curtain, had we wished to, and the resultant gain in speed was of enormous value to the show."

"About the show itself, I think the only thing I need say is that Alan Dent, then Dramatic critic for Punch, who took the trouble to come up to see it, said in his Punch notice: "The production of the Shakespeare tragedy – and we say it deliberately – was the best production of the play we have ever set eyes on.""

Clare Harris remained with the Wilson Barrett company until her death from cancer in 1949. She had considerable success as an actress in London productions, prior to her joining the Wilson Barrett company; and her last stage appearance was in the London production of a big American success 'Family Portrait' with Fay Compton in 1948.

'Time and Chance' saw her arrival in Edinburgh as a life saving factor in the history of the Wilson Barrett company for which he was deeply grateful. He wrote, "For the next five years I never had to think about the production side of the theatre at all. I knew that if I went away for ten years, when I came back I should find everyone happy and the standard higher than when I left. *It is saddening to think how very few people one comes across, in a lifetime of work, in whom one can place utter and complete confidence. Brilliant workmen, yes, there is no lack of these, but so often they are warped in some way, or subordinate everything to their own fierce personal ambition.* Clare, from the very start, considered only what she felt was best for the company, and as the years passed and the company, both as a whole and individually, became dearer to her, this consideration was paramount with her in every phase of her life and work."

We have noticed one theatre family, the Salbergs of Birmingham, who offered good, and on occasions, excellent entertainment at the Alexandra theatre, being labelled as 'commercial' and from time to time Wilson Barrett was subject to this kind of criticism. He was an idealist who embodied the truth of

Dostoevsky's statement that "Ideals are pitiless". He worked harder than anyone else to create a fine team of actors presenting plays, that the majority of the playgoers of Edinburgh, enjoyed.

It was during one of these fashionable attacks on his Lyceum programme; usually taking the form of letters to The Scotsman, that he was given support from an unexpected source. In his own words, "We were defended most vigorously in the next issue of The Scotsman by no less a person than our greatest Shakespearean authority, Professor Dover Wilson. I wrote to thank him for his championship, and was delighted to find that he and his wife were permanent bookers."

Besides Clare Harris, in 1948 he employed another producer, namely Joan Kemp-Welch, who was to produce 250 plays for the company; followed by a distinctive career as a freelance director for theatre, films, and TV productions. Her awards include: TV Oscar for Light Entertainment for Cool for Cats, 1958; Silver Dove UNNRA for Ballet, Laudes Evangeli, 1962;

Illustration 11.2 Clare Harris, producer for Wilson Barrett

and Prix Italia for The Lover, 1963; Desmond David Award for her services to television, 1963; Wilkie Baird award for creative work on TV; productions include: The Birthday Party, A View From the Bridge, A Midsummer Night's Dream.

Of Wilson Barrett she writes, "A truly great theatre personality – he gave his life to the theatre and the theatre was his life – he ran the company with authority but had the ability to make everyone feel part of a family and indeed we still do – only two Rep companies in my life had this lasting effect on actors who had worked there, one was the W. B. company and the other Colchester. Wilson Barrett was remarkable in that when he was rehearsing a play or performing, though he was everyones' employer and boss, he always behaved as if he was just an actor. He would take any criticism and observe every note. He was first to arrive and was one of the hardest workers I have ever met and a joy to work with. He had a great knowledge about period costumes and had amassed a vast wardrobe and he saw that every costume was right to the last detail. He was also a very generous man and loved entertaining. His only passion, apart from the theatre, was his garden which was truly beautiful." [1]

I have listed 250 towns in England, Scotland, and Wales where Weekly Reps were to be found at some time between 1915 and 1965. I have given, so far, accounts of Weekly Reps that are reasonably well documented, and exemplify the three main categories of their initiation and development.

It would be tedious to attempt descriptions of all of them and, in some cases, even where the Rep ran for more than 10 years, there is little detailed documentation. Many of the towns were offered entertainment by the impresarios whom I present in Chapter 19, but the following are some, no less important to the theatregoers and supporters of 'their Rep'.

---

[1] Letter to Author

Chapter 12

Morecambe
[1925-55]

The mention of Morecambe Royalty theatre usually evokes the response 'Oh yes – Thora Hird!' One willingly concedes that this fine actress deserves her fame; but when you ask for another famous name who started his, or her career at Morecambe there is usually no definite response. I have mentioned Robert Stephens in the introduction. Geoffrey Kendal, the author of 'Shakespeare Wallah', was also there in the early days of his career.

The situation today, in the provincial Repertory theatres, seems to be that it is necessary to have someone well known on TV or films, in the caste; to attract an audience.

John Heath wrote, "Stars were not allowed at the Royalty but if they were, young Thora Hird would have been the star."

However, he does point out that in the variety theatre at Morecambe one went to see 'star performers' as well as the 'up and coming' ones. He writes, "During my boyhood and youth, I lived with my two aunts in a confectionery shop in Queen Street, Morecambe. During the 1930's and up to the mid-forties, we went every Monday night to the Winter Gardens Theatre to see all the top-line stars and every Wednesday night to the Royalty Theatre to see the plays. These were the highlights of each week and we all looked forward to our visits to the theatre. The Royalty Theatre was a repertory theatre which meant the players performed a play one week whilst at the same time learning the script and rehearsing for the following week's play. The excellence of their performances were proof of their professionalism. The Royalty was a much more intimate theatre than the Winter Gardens which held 3,500 people, one of the largest theatres in the country and had a full band – Reg Fisher and his Band. I always insisted on being seated $1/_2$ hour before the show started in order not to miss the overture of this resident band, whereas the Royalty had a three

Illustration 12.1 The Players and Staff 1926

Illustration 12.2 The Players past and present 1946

"I find it so hard to describe what I mean by a good actor. More often than not, it is someone who looks rather unpromising, humdrum and obscure when you meet them off stage. They are the people who are transfigured by the process of becoming someone else."…. Johnathan Miller in 'Subsequent Performances'. The above is hardly what Dr. Miller had in mind! … but it would apply.

piece band only, a piano, a violin and a cello, but the sound of that seemed more in keeping with a playhouse in a small intimate atmosphere. Although small, the auditorium was filled with carved veneer wood and the ceiling with carved cherubs. No expense had been spared on the interior. It was a beautiful little theatre and I was very sad when it was destroyed to make way for an Arndale shopping centre.

I am grateful to Thora Hird for the following, "How can anyone be anything but grateful for having been in 'Rep' – "forgetting last week's script – remembering this week's and learning next week's" – looking through one's theatrical hamper for some-thing to wear – lending things – borrowing things. My first payment for a performance was £1 – I played the 'echo' twin in Eden Philpotts 'Yellow Sands' – I really didn't need to study my lines because providing the other twin knew and said hers, I only had to echo the last half of the line!

It was whilst I was playing in 'Rep' in a play called 'As you Are' that George Formby saw me and arranged for me to go to Ealing Studios to be tested for the same part in the film. I didn't get the part – I was too young (the only time I was ever told I was too young!) but I was put under contract to Ealing Film Studios, which put me on the road to a very happy working life. That was in 1940! I'm still learning lines!" [1]

---

[1] Letter to Author.

Chapter 13

Croydon
[1931-59]

The Repertory theatres, nearer to London, before the 1939-45 war, included Croydon, which gave early theatrical experience to some who became well known – John Le Mesurier was one and he did not enjoy his Weekly Rep experience at Oldham, Sheffield, and Croydon. In his autobiography 'A Jobbing Actor' [1984] he says, "When nostalgia addicts regret the passing of weekly or bi-weekly Rep., I do wish they would remember how bad performances can be under those conditions." Had he said "some performances" one would not dispute this, but I think I have produced sufficient evidence to show that 'some performances' could be of a high standard.

In 1938 'Theatre World' ran a series on Repertory theatres and George Fearon wrote, "The romance of Croydon started in 1931 with the Greyhound Theatre, sponsored by Messrs Barclay Perkins, and when that venture closed down, the enthusiasm of Mr Somerville and his colleagues saw to it that a little hall, belonging to Ruskin House, was changed into a theatre. If I know anything about Mr Somerville he will not rest content till a bigger and better theatre has been erected. The demand is obviously there, but these things always take time.

After the Greyhound was closed it took about twelve months to get enough money together to commence the present venture in 1933. Nothing was considered too small an amount. The poor gave their sixpences and the rich their pounds and this spirit of self–sacrifice is still prominent in a town which, one day, will reap a rich harvest by the possession of a larger and more practicable repertory theatre than the one which exists today."

J. Baxter-Somerville (what a fine theatrical sounding name that is!) was a south coast lawyer who made enough money to indulge his passion for the theatre. He engaged John Le Mesurier at £5 a week. We have already met one impression of

Croydon Rep during the thirties, in Janet Burnell's recollection (see Coventry Rep Chapter 8). He writes, "On first acquaintance, the Croydon Rep was a great disappointment. Built to the specifications of a second rank village hall, it offended me, like the more grandly named Palladium in Edinburgh, by not having a stage door. You cannot imagine how I longed to achieve the kudos of collecting my dressing room key from an honest to goodness stage door keeper who would remember my name, tell me if there were any messages and generally make me feel as if I was needed about the place. By comparison, all other defects of the establishment paled into insignificance, including the stage (the size of postage stamp) and the two potting shed dressing rooms (a sort of 'his' and 'hers' arrangement).

But the people were something else again. Either JB was a good talent spotter or Croydon Rep was a first class training ground. Probably it was a bit of both. Judge for yourself from an honours board that includes Dennis Price, Mark Dignam, Maurice Denham and Carla Lehmann."

After the 1939-45 war the Croydon Rep was to be found at the Grand Theatre performing on a weekly change basis, and attracting a loyal following, perhaps best exemplified by Audrey Botting who, amongst others, replying to my request for 'memories and impressions' wrote, "I was interested to hear that you are researching into weekly rep., and was reminded of my introduction to the joys of the professional theatre from my visits to the Grand Theatre here in Croydon. I was only a schoolgirl at the time and my mother knew one of the lady usherettes who used to let us have her two complimentary tickets for Tuesday nights (always renowned as the most difficult night to fill any theatre). I can remember to this day the excitement of arriving at the theatre, with its Victorian interior, and the anticipation of the play to come. The theatre had its own smell; I still don't know what it was – but I would recognise it anywhere. I wonder what it was! One got to know and love the players. Last week's Important Earnest was this week's Hercule Poirot – I knew Edward Woodward when he was just a butler you know!

You have no doubt already heard from others that the Grand was built in 1896 and pulled down in 1959 to make way for concrete blocks and ugly flyovers. To me, and many hundreds of others, it was a sad day.

121

As a founder member of the Ashcroft Theatre Club, housed in the Fairfield Hall complex, my love of the theatre has not diminished but I still lament the passing of the dear old weekly rep at the Grand."

Valerie Portwin, emphasising the fact that one could have 'school girl crushes' on the players wrote, "From 1952-1959 my sister and I visited the Grand Theatre, Croydon, most Saturdays at the cost of 1/-d in the Gods – stone slabs with a thin layer of carpet. We attended the 5 o'clock performance and if we enjoyed the play, we also stayed on for the 8 o'clock showing – in our early teens we each had 'crushes' on certain of the males."

These included Leslie Phillips, Patrick Cargill, Shaun Sutton, Anthony Nicholls, Alan Wheatley, Mark Dignam, James Mason, Herbert Gregg and Wilfred Lawson.

Another correspondent – Frances Gillespie – remembered the thirties companies and her sister who made costumes for them. She states, "I remember the Croydon Rep which was in Ruskin House which was then somewhere between Lansdowne Road and Sydenham Road.They used to have a play on and be rehearsing next weeks at the same time. My older sister had her own dressmaking business and used to make the costumes for them.I was apprenticed to a photographer but on Saturdays I used to help her with the hemming and felling and then deliver the costumes to the theatre.

I met Emlyn Williams and Joyce Grenfell when they were unknowns.There was a young lady who worked there sometimes making stage shoes, she was the half sister of the musician Moisevitch and used to tell us tales of him and their family. They used to pull my leg a bit, they thought I was a bit prim, but in 1936 a fifteen year old was expected to be like that. They all seemed a bit potty to me but they were a cheery lot. I don't think the company in general had much money. The drawings for the clothes seemed very good but were often made of strange fabrics, Turkish towelling I remember once for economy's sake."

Chapter 14

Worthing
[1932-64]

Thirty miles further south, and by the sea, there was a thriving weekly Rep at Worthing which began in the early thirties. A correspondent recalls, "The company was called The Worthing Repertory Company and was managed by a Mr Charles Bell and W. Simson Fraser. Mr Bell was the manager and Mr Fraser an actor who has since become very widely known on TV as 'Smudge' in The Army Game.The company first started in a hall above some shops in the main road and then when the cinema near them became vacant, they took possession. The programmes were changed each week, we had drama, comedy, thrillers, Shakespeare, you name it, they did it, and jolly good they were too." She also remarked "I remember 'Sailor Beware' which became a hit and launched Peggy Mount on the road to stardom."

The story of 'Rep' in Worthing follows a, by now, familiar pattern. The enthusiasm and hard work of those who pioneered the venture, and the subsequent periods of regular support along with those when this was not so evident.

In a publication of 1985 entitled 'Worthing Theatre 1780-1984' by D. Robert Elleray, ALA, FRSA, he states, "On June 22, 1932, a four month licence for the theatre was granted to Charles William Bell and a permanent theatre had been established for Worthing. On July 4 the theatre re-opened with the Phoenix Players in 'Peg O' My Heart' and continued until late October with a well chosen sequence of plays, then, after a week's break, the 'Mask Players' put on 'By Candle Light'. and Bell was joined by W. Simson Fraser, whom he had met at the Lyric, Hammersmith, in 1930. Their subsequent partnership, the press commented "in the face of most discouraging circumstances... has not only established a reputation for the artistic quality of their productions allied to their wise selection of plays... but also built up an enthusiastic and regular audience".

In 1935 four years' hard work by the company was rewarded when the owner of the Picturedrome Cinema, Carl A. Seebold, put up about £60,000 for the conversion of the building into a theatre. The new theatre consisted of the refurbished auditorium of the Picturedrome, plus a grand new entrance and foyer, with a lounge and cocktail bar above on the north side. The designs of the new Union Place facade were by the local architect A.W.T. Goldsmith and very much in the contemporary 'deco' style of the mid-1930s. The 900 seat New Connaught Theatre opened on September 30 1935, with a performance of 'Theatre Royal' by Edna Ferber and George Kaufman. A rapturous reception was given to the new venture and it was reported that around 5,000 applications for the first night had been received."

I am indebted to Mrs J.V. Allen, whose sister was, for 17 years, the Box Office Manageress, for the following comments, "When she commenced work at the theatre in 1948 it was, for 18 months to two years, controlled by the Rank Organisation and was then taken over by a consortium of small businessmen, the late Melville Gillam being Managing Director. It was run as a weekly repertory theatre, the company rehearsing from Tuesday to Friday, having Thursday afternoons free (on one of which Warren Mitchell and his wife secretly married in Worthing whilst members of the company). They rehearsed from Tuesday to Saturday lunchtime for the next week's play, the dress rehearsal for that being on Monday afternoon in preparation for performances from Monday to Saturday evenings, with matinee performances on Wednesdays and Saturdays.

At the same time, the company were learning the play for the following week. After the Saturday evening performance, the scenery was dismantled for the current play and erected for the performance commencing the following Monday.

The Christmas pantomime commenced each Boxing Day, running for three weeks, twice daily. These were most beautifully dressed with costumes made by the theatre's own wardrobe mistress and her staff using extremely expensive materials. These pantomimes always had at least one very well known performer in the cast, usually as 'Dames', a few of these being Dennis Noble, Frederick Jaeger (who was also, at one time, a resident member of the theatre company), Gary Miller, Mark

Wynter, Alma Cogan (who was a Worthing girl and incidentally, attended Worthing Art College at the same time as my sister) and many more."

She recalls the visit in October 1958 of a distinguished Prime Minister, and his wife, to see their daughter in Terence Rattigan's 'Variations on a Theme', produced by Guy Vaesen "Sarah Churchill appeared in a play at the Connaught with Sir Winston and Lady Churchill attending the Friday evening performance (we have a photograph which appeared in the Worthing papers showing my mother and sister sitting in front of Sir Winston and Lady Churchill).

Diana Dors was another who appeared in a play one week. The theatre ran a 'Theatre club' which met on a Sunday evening each month in the theatre bar when the company, and club members who were made up of the regular theatre-goers, met to discuss the plays and the theatre generally on an informal and friendly basis. This gave the players and audience an opportunity of meeting each other. The Saturday evening performance was almost a 'Club' in itself as many of the seats were 'permanent bookings' with the result one sat every week with the same group of people becoming very friendly with each other. My own seat, for many years, was 'A4'. I have many of the original programmes which make very interesting reading especially as some now very well-known names appear in these in extremely small print!

Finally, as a matter of interest, I list below just some of the now well-known actors who either commenced their careers with the Connaught company or appeared with them very early in their careers:

Peter Byrne, Richard Coleman, Gerald Flood, Terence Alexander, Terence Morgan, Harold Pinter, Francis Matthews, Angela Browne, Suzanna York, Zena Marshall, Sarah Miles, Anthony Steele, Bill Travers, Gordon Jackson, Michael Craig, Leslie Crowther, Ted Rogers, Robin Bailey, Dinsdale Landen, Frederick Jaeger, Lyndon Brook, Faith Brook, Clive Francis, Andrew Sachs, John Le Messurier, Michael Bates, Brook Williams, Michael Lees, Barbara Murray, Peggy Mount, Patricia Routledge, Caroline Blakiston, Pamela Charles, Ian Holm (whose family were Worthing people), Simon Williams, Ronald Lewis, John Standing (Sir John Leon),

Renee Asherson, Edward Judd, Warren Mitchell, Anthony Bate, Hazel Bainbridge (whose daughters, Kate O'Mara and Belinda Carroll attended school in Worthing) and many, many others.

Some of the producers were Jack Williams, Terence Dudley, Alan Bridges (who was also an actor in the company).

Among some other artistes who made guest appearances were Jack Buchanan, Elsie Randolph, A.E. Matthews, Bobby Howes and Lupino Lane.

Often, at a Saturday evening performance there were as many 'names' in the audience as there were on stage, Stanley Baker, James Mason, Donald Sinden, Robin Maugham and John Mills attending at various times.

Chapter 15

Sheffield
[1923-45]

Sheffield Rep owed its initial impetus to the enthusiasm and hard work of Herbert Prentice, already mentioned in connection with Northampton Rep.

His early productions were with amateurs; and these stimulated enough interest for a group of local business and professional people to form an Executive Committee. These early days have been recorded by T. Alec Seed in his book 'The Sheffield Repertory Company'. He states, "A meeting held at the Y.M.C.A. in October 1923 marks the real beginning of the independent Sheffield Repertory Company. An Executive Committee was formed consisting of Wilfred Vickers, M.Sc., M.Ed. (Chairman), W.C. Landon (Treasurer), C.V. McNally (Secretary), A. Ballard, H.W.D. Harkcom and Herbert M. Prentice, who had given up his post with the Railway Company in order to devote the whole of his time, professionally, to play production. The subscription was 3/6d per annum.

The objects of the company were:
1. To promote and encourage interest in the Drama and kindred Arts.
2. To produce plays.
3. To arrange lectures, recitals, play-readings and discussions.
4. To promote social intercourse amongst the members.
5. To form a library of dramatic literature for the use of members.
6. The establishment of a permanent Repertory Theatre in Sheffield.

Amongst the names of those who served on the Executive Committee one finds Professors C.H. Desch, A.E. Morgan, and later Professors G. Bullough and B. Ifor Evans, which suggests that 'town and gown', in this University at least, could work together for a common cause; and it is unlikely that these academics would have given their support to a merely commercial set up, in the sense of being a company that existed to make money with the sole purpose of enriching a few individual promoters.

Anyway, the records show that in those early pioneer days no surplus of money was available. Losses on all of the productions was recorded. This was still an amateur company and, consequently, no wages had to be paid. That they continued to produce plays was due mainly to the enthusiasm of Herbert and Marion Prentice. The anxiety was only relieved when it was known that 'Mr Prentice has had tea with Miss....', It is no surprise to read that on the 8th October 1921, a shockingly wet day, they had a Flag Day by which they raised £125.

In 1924 the company moved to new premises in South Street. 'The plan was to open with 'The Romantic Young Lady' by G. Martinez Sierra on 23rd June 1924. The schoolroom held 240 in the saloon and 190 in the balcony. The saloon prices were fixed at 8d and 1/2d and those in the balcony at 2/4d and 3/6d.

Illustration 15.1 Herbert and Marion Prentice working at Southport, 1942

Cushions were provided for the 3/6d seats. The membership rose from 77 in January to 160 in June but this was nothing like sufficient to cover the costs involved. The initial expenses at South Street were £120 and the Minutes record the first warning of the Chairman that the Company might have to close down."

Oh dear! This is still a familiar cry today, the difference being that today the theatre is reliant on public funding through the local authority and the Arts Council.

In May, 1928, the company moved again to premises in Townhead Street. Illustration 15.2 indicates that this building was not a purpose built theatre, though there could be no doubt as to its purpose as a Repertory Theatre! Some might comment that the play 'Square Pegs', being advertised, was very appropriate in the sense that weekly Rep was always trying to fit a square peg into a round hole! This theatre was completely reconstructed in 1953.

The Executive Committee decided, in 1936, to convert the Sheffield Rep Company into a wholly professional non-profit

Illustration 15.2 Entrance to the old Repertory Theatre, Townhead Street, Sheffield, 1945

distributing theatre.

A producer and seven professionals were engaged, and it was decided that there should be a change of production every week.

This scheme proved to be one of the most important in the history of the Rep Co. Its immediate effect was to turn a loss of £35 in 1935 into a profit of £1,353 in 1936.

During the war [1939-45] the theatre was closed but the Sheffield Rep Co., managed to find a new home at Southport. Geoffrey Ost, who was appointed producer in 1938, managed to establish a good relationship with the theatre enthusiasts of Southport, and when he was called up for the forces in 1942, Herbert Prentice returned, after an absence of sixteen years, as producer. Geoffrey Ost, was an outstanding man of repertory theatre, but apart from the first year or two at Sheffield, he was involved with fortnightly Rep.

H. Prentice was a singularly significant figure in the development of Rep in this country.

An enthusiastic amateur he was employed by the Great Central Railway Co., and Alec Seed writes, "In 1919 Herbert M. Prentice, who was employed on a scholarship training course with the Great Central Railway Company, and his wife, Marion, went to live at the Hostel of the Settlement, and one night over dinner they discussed drama and the theatre with friends and decided they would 'do' a play at the Settlement itself. Herbert Prentice continued with his work on the railway but his heart was in the theatre. A man of impeccable artistic taste, with great ideas and enthusiasm with which he was able to inspire his friends".

He continued to develop his own skills, mainly as a producer, until he left the company in 1926 to produce for Terence Gray at the Cambridge Festival theatre. Alec Seed wrote the following tribute: "It is perhaps, right to record here that his great work was achieved in the face of overwhelming difficulties, both financial and practical. At first he not only chose the plays but produced them, acted in them, and designed and made the scenery for them. In this he was supported by a body of amateurs who regarded him, some with awe and some with a very great affection. As an idealist he felt that he was always hampered by a Committee which had not the knowledge of the theatre necessary for its administration. The whole edifice at one time rested on his shoulders. He saved it again and again from bankruptcy and only by his perseverance and skill was the Company kept alive. A Producer can only do his best work when not burdened with business worries and, up to his leaving for Cambridge, Herbert Prentice never had this freedom. A review of the Press notices of his productions, however, gives no hint that his work suffered. When he returned, after sixteen years, to produce, first at Southport and then at Sheffield, not only had his skill developed but, freed from financial and business problems, he gave some magnificent productions which attracted audiences from far and wide."

It was typical of his self effacing behaviour that, after five years of producing at The Festival Theatre, Cambridge; four years (weekly Rep) at Northampton, where he did 200 productions, with settings by Tom Osborne Robinson, and eight years at Birmingham Rep; when he returned to Sheffield in 1945 he was quite prepared to help with the more unpleasant business of tidying up the theatre after war time use. Alec Seed records, "Almost everything required renewing, including scenery and seats, and the place had become a deposit for junk of all kinds. Herbert Prentice was brought over from Southport as Director–Producer but before a production could be staged there was four months gruelling work, clearing rubbish away, sorting out what was useful and what was not, painting, repairing, renewing electric cables and all manner of jobs. The balcony (as it was then called) was re-floored and the old cinema projecting box removed and the whole of the auditorium was repainted. Fortunately, it was now possible to get materials more readily, but the accomplishment of the task of re-opening in 1945 may be regarded as one of the major accomplishments in the Company's history.

(Herbert Prentice and I spent every night and every weekend sorting, repairing, painting.... doing anything. Both well remember painting a ceiling, one from either side, chatting away to each other in good spirits. By the time we met in the centre we were not on speaking terms!)"

During the twenties, when young John C. Trewin was making his way through the streets of Plymouth, to see the plays presented by Geo. S. King, on a weekly change basis; nearly 300 miles further north, another young man was making his way through the back streets of Sheffield to witness the early efforts of an actor who was to become an outstanding Shakespearean one. The young man's name was Harold Hobson, and Donald Wolfit, the name of the actor.

Recalling those days Harold Hobson, in a letter written to Donald in 1949 wrote: "Memories of the superb performances which you gave in the 1920s, at the Sheffield Repertory Theatre, are still fresh in my mind. Often I think of how I used to walk home to Nether Edge, excited, exalted, and aglow, after some performance of yours in Shaw, Galsworthy or Barrie."

Later, about those same performances:

"I was as much moved by some of them as I have ever been by any actor in the theatre." [1]

---

[1] 'Sir Donald Wolfit' by Ronald Harwood [1971]

Chapter 16

Perth
[1935-46]

Repertory at Perth, as with so many companies, began with the enthusiasm of two young people, namely, David Steuart and Marjorie Dence.

In the early thirties they met when playing together with the London University Drama Society, and with the Greater London Players. In an interview with William Kemp, who was for 30 years correspondent to 'The Stage' newspaper, Marjorie Dence explained how it all began.

"One night, after a performance in the Town Hall, Ilford, we were waiting together on the station for the last train back to town. On the station wall was a map of Scotland. David Steuart pointed to Perth and remarked, "That's where I'm going to run a repertory theatre one day. I believe they have practically nothing in the way of live theatre except in the big cities." The train came in and we pursued our respective ways home and forgot the conversation. A few days later, I was sitting at breakfast with my family reading the theatrical newspaper 'The Stage'. In it was an advertisement of a theatre for sale in Perth. I remarked casually that that was where David Steuart wanted to run a theatre and my father made the astounding and totally unexpected offer that if David Steuart and I thought we could make a success of it he was willing to investigate the possibility of acquiring the building. And it all followed from that."

On September 23rd, 1935, the new repertory company opened with a play about Henry VIII 'The Rose Without a Thorn' by Clifford Bax.

The years that followed saw periods of mild prosperity and those of considerable difficulties, but rarely of despair.

There was a period, during the war, when it looked as though they would have to close, and I think Marjorie Dence's description of the outcome is worth quoting in full when, in these days of subsidy, things may be too easily taken for granted.

"Finally we made up our minds to pay the company off and send them back to their homes. Then, almost as we came to this decision, news arrived that theatres might re-open at the end of that week. Someone suddenly made a suggestion that seemed to bring a ray of hope. We could not face further financial loss. All right! There must be no financial loss. Why not run the theatre on a profit-sharing, communal basis? The company were consulted and most of them readily agreed to try out the scheme and once more there seemed to be a hope of continuing our work. The new scheme was roughly as follows:- we would cut expenses to a minimum, sharing such work as box office, theatre cleaning, scene shifting, etc, between us. We would provide all members of the company with board and lodging, and at the end of each week, after paying all our expenses, we would divide among us what remained. How well I remember the weekly share-out. Often it was little more than a few shillings. If the play had been a winner it might rise to as much as £5 each. To begin with we had to feel our way very carefully. We made dormitories for the members of the company in the theatre; a cook was engaged and meals were cooked and eaten in the theatre coffee bar. A rota of work was carefully thought out, and we all consulted the lists to see whose turn it was to sweep the theatre or attend to the box office. Programme selling and coffee bar attendance were done voluntarily by kind friends of the theatre. Later as, things sorted themselves out, we began to know better what we could do. We found we could afford to have some front of house staff, and every one was glad to be quit of their cleaning duties. Then it was felt that the smell of our supper cooking was apt to permeate the auditorium, and we moved to a basement kitchen kindly lent to us by one of the theatre friends. A gypsy sort of life it was, but somehow there was a grand sense of comradeship. Just because the living conditions were so hard and the financial rewards so negligible, we attracted only people with the right spirit, who were keen on the work for its own sake. We also felt that we were doing something to save our beloved theatre from extinction, besides bringing some brightness to the lives of our audiences at a time when it was badly needed."

Looking back over a long life in the theatre, David Steuart, in his 80th year, was asked the inevitable question, "was it a treadmill existence doing weekly rep for 52 weeks a year? "No!

It was never that. It never did become routine and there was always an excitement with every new production. Good heavens, we found time to enjoy ourselves. I recall tennis parties and afternoon teas. Climbing Schiehallion at midsummer and walking Ben-y-Vrackie."

Chapter 17

Oldham
[1938-68]

Repertory in Oldham has a long and varied history. Oldham, as with many other towns, had more than one theatre putting on 'straight' plays; but the development of a repertory company, of long standing, was to be found at the Coliseum theatre. (The original spelling was Colosseum but due to a printing error this became Coliseum, and has been retained to this day).

The original building was made of wood, and it is remarkable that the place was not burnt down. Today, with the easy access to a vast public, of political opinion, by way of television, we tend to forget that, prior to this, political parties had to rely on public halls, and theatre, in which to present the then 'personalities' of their party. The Coliseum was no exception. Janet Greaves, in her account of Oldham's Theatre writes, "People would queue for hours to get into the hall or theatre which would be filled to capacity. There would often be an overflowing meeting in some smaller nearby hall, and still there would frequently be people left out in the street. I remember once being almost crushed to pulp when I became wrapped around one of the pillars at the entrance to the Coliseum with hundreds of people flattening me out. I felt like the jam in a raspberry roll. To the Coliseum came J. R. Clynes, Lloyd George and Ramsey MacDonald, together with scores of others with only slightly less well-known names."

It stood empty for seven years during the thirties and it was during the latter part of this decade that, thanks to the initiative of a young theatre enthusiast named Joe Holroyd, the movement towards a permanent repertory company was made.

He was a regular attender at the Grand Theatre in the early thirties, when the Terence Byron Repertory company performed on a twice nightly basis. The opportunity to fulfil his desire to 'tread the boards' of the live theatre came when he saw a notice saying that extras were required for a play. In his own words, "Among the special attractions staged by the repertory company was 'Ambrose Applejohn's Adventure', and it was announced that they were looking for extras to be the pirates. I applied, and to my great delight was accepted. So, for one glorious week I tried to look like a fierce pirate – eye patch and all. The wages were a 20 packet of cigarettes, but the real thrill was in meeting real actors for the first time."

It was a sad day for him when it was announced that, after three years, the T. Byron company, would have to finish. However, whether it was due to excessive optimism, or blind ignorance, there was always another impresario willing to risk his money in the repertory theatre, and W. Armitage Owen (for long the manager of the Manchester [Rusholme] Repertory company) presented one of his companies at the Grand. Another letter to the local paper appealing for all playgoers to pool their enthusiasm, and ideas, saw the formation of the Oldham Playgoer's club.

This was the start of a venture that was to continue for many years. The failure of the impresarios to attract sufficient support at the Grand and Theatre Royal, saw the Playgoers' club hiring the Temperance Hall and, on January 30th 1938, the Rep opened with Shaw's 'Arms and the Man'. Janet Greaves records, "Life was not easy. There was only a wooden partition between the foyer where refreshments were prepared and the auditorium where both actors and audience could hear the slightest tinkle of a coffee spoon. Also it was cold; coconut matting between the rows did little to thaw the frozen feet of the patrons. Moreover, on the opening night there was an almighty storm calculated to keep anyone but the most ardent theatre-lover away from a cold and draughty building. Yet the membership list grew longer and longer. Whilst the Theatre Royal and the Empire struggled in vain to keep their doors open, the queues for the Rep wound their way around the streets.Three months after opening, this list had reached 2,000 and the Temperance Hall was already so inadequate that efforts were made to find larger accommodation. This was found in the shabby, neglected Colosseum, lying under seven years of dirt and without a floor, but it was a theatre, had been built as a theatre, and was one, moreover, with a history. A lease was taken out, £700 spent to make the place habitable and the move was made in July 1939. After eighteen months in the

Temperance Hall the company closed there with 'Lot's wife', and the singing of Auld Lang Syne. Two days later, on the following Monday, the Colosseum opened with 'Poison Pen'. Town officials were in the audience and a bouquet was presented to each actress. By this time the membership had reached 3,500. Incidentally, the name Colosseum was accidentally changed to Coliseum and retained. Meanwhile the Temperance Hall continued to be rented, as a workshop for the making of scenery, and was bought at some stage by the Rep.

So the dreams of the playgoers, particularly of those young, enthusiastic intrepid ones – young folk who would rush in when more mature angels would fear to tread – this dream had been realised; Oldham had a theatre, it was now the responsibility of the townspeople to see that it stayed alive and of a high standard."

Apart from John Barrie, other well known actors played there during the weekly change years.

The following are taken from 'The First Hundred Years' by James Carter (1986), the story of the Oldham Coliseum.

"I have many happy memories of my beginnings as an actor at the Coliseum under the gentle care of Douglas Emery who 'discovered' me. I hope the Coliseum continues to encourage young actors and to entertain audiences for many more years."

Bernard Cribbins

"The happiest days of my career were at 'the Rep'. I wish that other actresses could have the opportunity that was given to me. What joyous memories I have of the Temperance Hall and the Coliseum. Long may it reign."

Dora Bryan

"Having met my wife at the Coliseum and brought up two children virtually within its walls, it will always have a place in my heart. Also, I promise you, nowhere in the British Isles will you find such warm, enthusiastic, honest audiences. If they love you, they really let you know... If they don't then they will certainly call a spade a shovel.

Here's to another hundred years."

Kenneth Alan Taylor
Artistic Director Nottingham Playhouse

"It was at the Coliseum that I was given my first chance to be a professional actor, and as it is almost forty years ago I feel that we both made the right choice. However, full of the arrogance of youth and a pocketful of demob money, I wasn't really particular whether they took me on or not. At that time I was determined to be a stand-up visual comic, fortunately for me they gave me a chance. As a matter of fact I shudder when I think how near Oldham Rep came to turning me down, had they done so, and with every justification, I might now be retired, having spent a boring frustrating life in a cotton mill."

Eric Sykes

Chapter 18

Amersham
[1936-46]

"It is the ordinary, small town, play per week system of repertory in England and Wales which has my sympathy. At the repertory theatres I visited this year – Newcastle-on-Tyne and York – and at those near London that I visit more often – Amersham in Bucks, Windsor in Berkshire, Colchester in Essex – they put on a new play every blessed week and seldom do a revival of one of their own productions unless it has been an inordinate success; I don't know how it is done; they don't know how it is done. Charming lady producers receive me gladly... but with 'tears in their eyes, distraction in their aspect' (as Hamlet said of the First Player). The lady, as like as not, has a pot of glue in one hand and a pot of paint in the other... but more seriously, if these gay, gallant and busy little theatres did nothing but makeshift, shimble-shamble productions, I certainly shouldn't go out of my way to visit them. I enjoy their work – and so do a vast amount of people... There is seething capital repertory activity going on all over the country. Just think of it and say, if you dare, that the theatre is dying, in London or out of it."

The above is from The Listener, September 16th, 1943, and is an extract from a broadcast by Alan Dent.

The lady, or, more likely, in this small theatre at Amersham, 'the ladies' with glue pot and paint brush would be Sally Latimer and Caryl Jenner, who for ten years, including the Second World War years, with varying fortunes, managed to keep this little theatre alive.

They opened on Boxing Night, 1936 with N. Coward's 'Hay Fever'. We are told, "In those days there was no lounge, and downstairs in the Company dressing-rooms beneath the stage there was no heating. The actors and actresses sat around one oil-stove, and made up in a broken mirror by the light of a solitary bulb. Together with Sally, these members of the company scrubbed the stage, built and painted the sets, stage-managed the shows, moved the scenary, did all the electrical work, made the costumes: in fact, they did everything there was to do in the theatre.

They worked for what could hardly be called a salary, and the foundations of the theatre were laid only because these people were willing to work night and day to make it a success. Sally and her husband threw into the venture all their money and their energy."

The plays they produced represented all kinds of dramatic expression. There was an unexpected boost to the number of playgoers during the second World War, when people were evacuated from London. The following is from an account of the Amersham Rep's tenth anniversary publication: "The audience changed from a nucleus of theatre-loving people from the locality to a cosmopolitan audience drawn from all walks of life, many of the members evacuated from London. Many who heard of the Playhouse for the first time said: "They say there's a Rep here. What on earth's a Rep, my dear? Amateurs, aren't they? And what sort of a show can they give, at those prices?" But these people, who had never seen a Rep before, came to the theatre because it meant a release from the worry and struggle of life for a few hours, and as a result were completely won over to the idea of 'Rep'. The same people today rise as warriors of old if they hear a word against what they all now regard as 'our' Rep!"

For some part of the year, and for the whole in a considerable number, a repertory company could be found operating on a weekly change of play basis.

I'm sure that those I have mentioned could be matched, at sometime or other in other towns. Derby, Hull, Leeds, Harrogate, Bolton, Wigan, Windsor, Brighton, Dundee, etc.; all had weekly repertory theatres (in some cases more than one) for some periods between 1915–65.

The support given, if any, by the civic authorities varied from theatre to theatre, and from town to town; but the majority would be companies provided by theatre impresarios, independent of public funding other than that received at the box office.

Chapter 19

'Uncle Tom Cobley and All ....'

"There was Alfred Denville, Harry Hanson, Frank Fortescue, Armitage Owen, Arthur Brough, Richard Burnett... Old Uncle Tom Cobley and all . . ."

Well, I am not aware that there was a Tom Cobley amongst the many impresarios, who presented plays on a weekly change basis, but I would not have been surprised had the name turned up!

The names above are some of those who would be better known to the actors seeking employment during the long period of the Weekly Reps.

A diverse and varied assortment in terms of their artistic perception, business integrity, and personality. No doubt some were the traditional 'rogues and vagabonds' of the theatre, but most seemed to have been persons with a genuine interest in the theatre as entertainment. When is theatre not entertainment is an interesting question. The programme planners for Radio 3 designate the time from 5.00 pm to 6.30 pm as being 'Mainly for Pleasure' implying that the rest of the day's plan is not!

The middle fifties saw the emergence of more plays, and players, from what is usually referred to as 'the working classes'. A term which I'm sure even the most bigoted left winger would concede does not denote all of those people who work for a living.

The quickest way to demean human beings is to lump them all together under a class label – the infinite variety of experience is not the preserve of any one group but belongs to the species 'human beings'. There are as many classes as there are human beings. [1]

These new enlighteners of our darkness used, and still use 'shock' tactics to arouse those whom they think need awakening from their complacency. (These, by the way, were, and still are, expected to pay for this therapeutic treatment).

One suspects that our 'shock troopers' would not be amongst

those willing to make the supreme sacrifice of allowing the suspension of 'pretending to be' to make way for their actual killing, where this is portrayed in one of their plays in which, he or she, plays the part – because they would not be around to observe the 'shock effect' of this novel way of committing suicide.

One cannot deny that the theatre can be the means of assembling powerful reminders that all is not well in this or that area of human activity; but if the plays then become the vehicle of political propaganda, of a one sided nature, then they cease to be drama.

Drama can be Aristocratic family v. Aristocratic family; Wicked capitalist bosses v. Down-trodden workers; Striking miners v. Non striking miners; Father v. Son; Daughter v. Mother; – the permutations are endless. The duration of a 'drama' can be anything from the 9-11 hours of Peter Brook's 'Mahabharata', to the ever diminishing time-span of a Samuel Beckett play.

G.B. Shaw's 'St. Joan' is drama because Shaw tried to be fair to all sides. A playwright may be as imbued with irrational hatred and loathing as anyone else, and he is at liberty to express this in his play; but he should not be surprised if people are disinclined to offer money to witness this or that portrayal of despair.

However, if you happen to believe that all of these unpleasant situations and conditions are due to capitalist society, and only when this has been eliminated can there be peace and harmony, then your plays will, inevitably, try to influence people to bring this about and, in a free society, this is permissible. Whether one should expect money from a Tory government, that supports capitalism, to enable one to present one's play, or plays, is a debatable issue.

To return to our impresarios – one thing is certain – none of them expected money to come from anywhere but their own pockets and the takings at the box office.

❑   Alfred Denville

In 1948 I joined a theatrical company, in Scotland, that performed under the name of The Kinloch Players. I had been advised by Geoffrey Staines; the producer at the York Repertory

theatre, with whom I discussed my desire to work in the theatre
– to take any job that was offered by a professional company
because it would be easier to obtain work elsewhere if you were
already engaged professionally.

I replied to an advert in 'The Stage' for someone to work with
The Kinlock Players, a touring company in Scotland and,
surprisingly, I was offered a job with a salary of £2 per week. I
decided to follow G. Staines' advice and accepted it.

Had I known what I was letting myself in for I would not have
gone and, no doubt, the whole course of my subsequent
experience would have been different. This was one occasion
when I'm glad I did not know.

One wet November morning I boarded a train in York and
travelled north to Falkirk; here I transferred to a bus going to
the village of Torphicen (near Bathgate). The bus stop was near
to the village hall where I had been told to report.

In one of the smaller rooms, adjoining the main hall, amongst
a quantity of skips full of costumes, I met Henry Parker and
Mary Kinloch. These were their stage names; they were married
and had a son who was doing his National Service and who,
when he was free at weekends, and stationed nearby, would
join his parents for the Saturday show.

The 'Saturday show'? Yes – Saturday night was the 'all
laughter' show. I discovered that I had joined a fit-up company
where a play, or entertainment of a different kind, was presented each evening – but never on Sunday!

It may be hard to believe now but we stayed for ten weeks in
one village, during the year I was with them. We were never
more than seven or eight, including Henry and Mary, and yet
we managed Cecil De Mille type productions with a cast of
thousands!

Well – that's how it seemed at times – one acted, made bits of
scenery, and attempted to memorise lines. These were on 'cue
sheets' – meaning that one did not have the whole of the
previous actor's speech – but only the last three or four words!

I remember 'under dressing' if one was playing two or three
parts in one play. There was no time for a complete change of
costume so one wore some of the last character to be portrayed
under part of the first and second! Rather like peeling an onion.

If we were doing 'East Lynne' – about 3.00 pm Henry would
exclaim "I must be off to kidnap a lad coming out of school to

play Little Willie'; and he would return with a willing candidate, (no Equity card!) who was quickly rehearsed, and who kept 'dead' still when Mary knelt and uttered those much parodied lines "Dead – dead – and never called me mother!" This was always received in silence – even a tear or two – something, no doubt, beyond the comprehension of the more sophisticated audience of today – which may only mean more 'head' and less 'heart'.

For 'Snow White' Henry would 'kidnap' seven kids; and this meant one was sure of forty, or more, in the audience, since, at least, half a dozen relatives, and friends, would come along to see 'their child' starring in this mammoth production. If business was very poor I'm sure Henry would have been tempted to put on 'Snow White and the Seventeen Dwarfs', but for the fact that the stage was not big enough to accomodate so many.

About this time the radio feature ITMA was still being broadcast and, when Henry appeared in the streets, the children would greet him with "It's that man again!" However, there was one exception to this, and Henry would make a special plea,

Illustration 19.1 The Kinloch Players – Friday night

145

from the stage on Saturday evening, that they would not shout this when, suitably attired, he would walk to the kirk on Sunday mornings; no doubt, and understandably, to ask the Lord's blessing on 'the good, wholesome family entertainment' which he offered to the public.

But I digress – this book is about the luxury of having a whole week in which to prepare a play, ("It just shows how relative everything is" said Alice), and not about the survival of a fit-up company in Scotland.

After I left them I often wondered what had become of them – they were not young in 1948. During my research the editor of 'The Stage' kindly published letters requesting information about 'Weekly Reps'; and one that I received amongst many, was written in a clear and comprehensive manner and signed Mary Kinloch Parker! My subsequent enquiry as to whether she was the Mary Kinloch of The Kinloch Players with whom I had been involved in 1948 (this was 1984); and in which I had remarked "you must be well over 21 now" brought the pleasing response that she was indeed the same and the observation

Illustration 19.2 The Kinloch Players – Saturday night

Illustration 19.3 A 'Kinloch Players' Poster
This was an exceptional week – no Saturday performance!

"you are right – I am well over 21 – I'm now over 91!" [2]
  I have been greatly helped in unearthing evidence of theatre
activities in the provinces by amateur theatre enthusiasts, who
on retirement, have occupied themselves by collecting information about the theatres, and their activities, in their own towns.
One such is Stanley Wild, of Macclesfield, in Cheshire. From
programmes he had retained he sent me the names of the
members of the Alfred Denville Stock Co., appearing at the
Opera House, Macclesfield in 1929, and amongst them I
spotted the names of Henry Parker and Mary Kinloch. A further
visit to his home to look at photographs and newspaper
cuttings, revealed the photo of the Denville Co., and Henry and
Mary can be seen on the front row standing to the right of the
lad wearing the 'long shorts'.
  Having no permanent home, and always living in 'digs', never
being sure how business would be; their life seemed, in
retrospect, a hard one. She comments, "As you say, perhaps
some people would call ours a hard life, but it was not to us, it
was very full and a successful and very happy marriage – 43
years. When we married we said we would not take separate

*Illustration 19.4 Alfred Denville Stock Company, Macclesfield
Opera House, 1929*

engagements and we did not – a few odd weeks, either one or the other and whoever wasn't working did the babysitting!! We retired in 1964 and have a lovely five room cottage here and a large garden. We did very well with The Kinloch Players after going north. Inverness, Elgin, Peterhead etc., we were before our time – we opened up places that have since become regular touring dates. I established a cottage industry and make patchwork cushions, tea cosies, aprons, bags etc. I had a buyer in a boutique in the Strand for fifteen years but they retired two years ago. I have made four bed covers and am now on the fifth."

So, when the Artistic Director of the National Theatre, and his fellow directors, are working away at their hand weaving loom to make cloth for costumes, because their grant is a million or two short – maybe they will spare a thought for these old troupers who kept the theatre alive on much less than the proverbial shoestring.

Regarding Alfred Denville, Mary wrote, "Alfred Denville was the premier weekly rep management in England, during his peak period he had more than twenty theatres going at the same time. From around 1920 all the companies averaged 16 artistes, plus a manager, carpenter, electrician and scenic artiste. The shows were first class and paid their way – no government or council grant in those days. After a year or more there was a short break and we started again with an interchange of company."

Alfred Denville was born in Nottingham on 28 January, 1876, and died 23 March 1955. He made his first stage appearance, when only four weeks old, when he was carried on at the Prince of Wales Theatre, Greenwich. In his earliest years he played children's parts in the company of his idol, the Famous Barry Sullivan. After a thorough grounding with such an experienced player, he went on tour with circuses; produced pantomimes at all the principal theatres, and was star comedian with Vezin in Shakespearean and classical comedies.

In his early twenties he formed his first company at Morriston, near Swansea; and from then on he had 160 companies operating, for various lengths of time, in theatres north and south. He was said to have had 25 companies on the road at the same time; and claimed to have played in every county except Rutland.

One interesting feature of his companies is that he continued to use the term 'Stock', rather than Repertory, though this term was generally associated with theatrical companies during the latter part of the 19th century and the early years of this one. We can see it on the photo of 1929; but as late as 1953 (two years before he died) he had a company, at the Coliseum Theatre, Harrow, which he built, under the title 'The Alfred Denville Stock Company'.

In 1917 he moved to Oldham where he took up residence in the town and had a company playing at the Theatre Royal until 1921.

He was an extraordinary energetic person and, apart from his interest in the theatre, he was concerned with social and political matters, which saw him being chosen as Conservative MP for Central Newcastle from 1931 until 1945. He became known as 'the Actors' MP.

In 1925 he gave Denville Hall, in Northwood, (Middlesex) as a house of rest for aged actors and actresses, and this is still fulfilling this useful purpose.

I am indebted to his grandson, Terence Denville, for the following comments on his grandfather. "My grandfather came from an acting family; he was one of thirteen children. His father was drowned when fairly young when out swimming with one John Latimer, who subsequently married the widow. (There was much speculation about this). The Latimers were often so hard up that, as they travelled about the country, they occasionally gave the odd child away to any landlady willing to take it. In his later years my grandfather made quite a hobby of trying to track down these lost brothers and sisters. I remember that one, Will, was a Durham coal miner. He was a fascinating, if rather terrifying man, and a most accomplished raconteur. If you were wise, you never believed one story in ten which he told about himself, but they were marvellous to listen to. He tried to claim great antiquity for the Denvilles ('descended, of course, from Dennaville, a jongleur who came over with the Conqueror') but, in fact, he assumed the name, his real name being Simons. His wife, Kate Saville, from whom he separated, really had a distinguished theatre pedigree; she was related to Kean in some way and two of her immediate forebears were Helena Fawcett and a well-known Victorian Kate Saville."

His son, Charles, who also had companies operating in provincial theatres, is remembered by Alice Favell. "More than

30 years ago my husband and I (yes – in spite of the address, in fact, we are convinced that all clergy ought to have a theatre background and training) as I was saying, we were in the professional theatre, in weekly rep, and true rep, and we worked for Charlie Denville at South Shields Pier Pavilion for about two years. CD (as he was called) was the most incredible character. I don't really know where to begin!! He was a real old–fashioned actor–manager. He was often tight and he could lose his temper dreadfully but he had a heart of gold (as the saying is) and we couldn't help being fond of him really. I was the scenic artiste, but one of my jobs was to go to the pub and get him a quarter bottle of rum, which he used to put in his tea, and then leave it on the piano! He liked all the sets to be designed exactly the same as they were when Alfred Denville produced the plays, which was of course a bit limiting. But every now and and then we would do a play which was not written in A. Denville's time and then we could go to town. The best compliment I ever had from him was when I did the set for 'Streetcar named Desire'. He said, "I tell you what – that's the Cat's Bloody Whiskers!" He also once described my husband as 'a Bloody Good Old Bloke", which was also a great compliment! As he got older he used to forget his lines and ad libbed dreadfully. The company found this most unnerving and dreaded shows that he acted in! Mrs Lily Denville too was a great character but she was most kind and we got on with her very well. I left them to have my first baby, and they gave me a beautiful christening shawl; which our subsequent children were christened in, and which I have still and will be carefully handed down.

He appears again in Kenneth More's book 'More or Less' as the Actor-Manager at the Grand Theatre, Byker, when they did, not one play a week, but two!

Terence Denville's comment again briefly sums up a rather sad, if not tragic, character. "Charles always tried, rather unsuccessfully, to imitate his father. He was a strange and rather sad figure. In his later years he was usually the worse for drink and was always inventing ways to send people out to buy him whisky without his rather prim wife, Lily, knowing. I heard her complain once that she had never realised how often it was necessary to hurry out for yet another pound of six-inch nails!"

151

❑   Harry Hanson

One of the longest running Weekly Rep companies was that of Harry Hanson's Court Players, at the Pier Pavilion Theatre, Hastings. This ran from 1933–64, averaging more than forty continuous weeks each year.

John Osborne's comments on this somewhat enigmatic character are quoted by Rowell and Jackson [1984] and, more surprisingly, in the excellent, and deeply researched book by M. Sanderson 'From Irving to Olivier' [1985].

J. Osborne says, "Hanson's companies were dreaded as the last funk–hole for any actor, but they were not easy to penetrate. If there was a Hanson kind of theatre, there was a Hanson kind of actor, unpersonable, defeated from the outset and grateful to have any sort of job at all. They were apologetic about themselves, if not among themselves. Equity representatives were unknown to speak, fluffs and dries were entered into a book by the stage director and other misdemeanours literally according to the Hanson Book. He was the theatre's Gradgrind and his theatres were administered like workhouses of despair..." ('A Better Class of Person' [1981])

Osborne, as usual, was dismissed after three months, and, as with many of our utterances, this perhaps tells us as much about him as about Harry Hanson.

Sanderson says, "At the top end of the spectrum of touring companies was Donald Wolfit". Somewhat lower down were companies like that of Harry Hanson, who ran half a dozen troupes and of whom J. Osborne says, "a byword for tatty ill-paid, tyrannical, joyless work."

Half a dozen companies? – more like twenty for most of the years between 1932 and 1965.

At the risk of sounding repetitive let me say again that it is mistaken to generalise about any theatre organisation, whether subsidised or non–subsidised.

The situation Osborne found at the Palace Theatre, Camberwell, may well have been a true description of that company, but my own experience, and that of other correspondents, was of an employer who paid as well as most theatrical employers, and whose companies varied over the long period in which they were to be found.

In a Silver Jubilee book we find, "He has been called the

'Woolworth of the Profession'. This would offend some men, but
not H.H. When it was first mentioned to him, he smiled rather
disarmingly and a little wickedly perhaps, and said "Yes, I like
that. Very nicely put, and very true". H.H. also said "I am a
shopkeeper, I sell plays. The customer is always right, and I
must try and understand the products they want."

Harry Hanson was born in March 1895. As a young man he
appeared with various 'stock' companies but we find him, in
1920, appearing as a speciality dancer in "Pick–a–Dilly" at the
London Pavilion; and this he continued to do until he went into
management in 1933. Apart from Hastings, he had other
permanent companies, and many seasonal ones.

Kenneth Watson managed the Peterborough company for
some years. He states, "We did have the benefit of being a year-
round resident company, we had an enormous stock of scenery, props and furniture which were not so readily available to
seasonal companies, albeit in bigger theatres, such as T.R.
Leeds, Alhambra, Bradford, and also Norwich, which you know
(my wife worked there for H.H. in 1952). Standards of productions varied considerably from theatre to theatre, depending a
lot on amount of scenery available and its nature – also the
scenic artist! – and the nature of the producer and actors. One
common factor, however, was discipline. Harry insisted on it
and producers and actors ignored it at their peril. Lines and
moves HAD to be known (absolutely no books after Friday) and
alcohol before or during the show was O—U—T. Breaking that
rule so as to affect performances led to the sack."

Members of theatre companies, that are almost wholly maintained by subsidy, can have little idea of what it means to exist
on box office takings only. That H. Hanson had two companies
(one at Hastings and another at Peterborough) that ran for over
thirty, and twenty years, respectively, on box office takings,
indicates that the entertainment offered was of a reasonable
standard.

How can one compare the 9–11 plays a year at the Royal
Exchange theatre, Manchester, where they are at present
receiving over a million pounds a year subsidy, with the
forty–five, on average, of many of the Weekly Reps? That the
former do the occasional first production, or that they can
afford to put on the occasional experimental play that will only
have minority appeal, is not denied. It would be interesting to

see a modern director's choice of forty–five plays for a year, followed by another forty–five each year for up to twenty years and more!

That some of the non–subsidised impresarios behaved, on occasions, in a somewhat ruthless manner is not denied, but this could be balanced with generosity to those who, in their estimation, served them well.

The following account by Philip Weathers seems to sum up H. Hanson better than most: "I first met him at the Pier Theatre, Hastings, about 1935. He was courteous and business-like. We kept in touch. Two or three years later he asked me to work for him. Whilst I got to know him better, there was never a personal friendship, and my impression is he was never personally friendly with anyone who worked for him, except the members of his first Court Players company at Hastings. He kept them in work, and helped them financially when they were unable to work either through illness or age. As against this he could be ruthless, cruel, when it suited him. Witness the severance of the relationship with the companion of many years, who had helped finance the early days – and the abrupt dismissal of a business manager who formerly had been one of his greatest mainstays. I never knew him to be rude or adversely critical to any of his artistes – to their face – behind their backs there could be waspish comments, usually very much to the point. He was mercurial, sometimes almost dancing with glee, as immediately after signing the big contract with George Black: at other times cold, uncommunicative, seemingly pessimistic. And minor physical ailments upset him inordinately. He never allowed these moods to hinder him working towards the fulfilment of his ambition. I was never certain what his final goal might be – possibly he wasn't either. Success, certainly, was vital to him, but he took failure philosophically. I doubt if the amassing of money was particularly important.

I lost touch for the six years of the war. I never heard of him making any attempt to keep contact with any former member of his companies in the Armed Forces. When I met him again much of the drive had gone, he seemed to be doing the 'right thing' mechanically, relying far more on competent employees than formerly, valuing his private life at Warlingham probably more than his public life in the theatre."

I am indebted to Colin Bean for the following comments, and

stories, about H. Hanson:

"Ever since Theatre School I've always been a Character Actor (to use that lovely old fashioned nomenclature). Make-up, wigs, noses, beards and disguises fascinate me. One week, during one of my Sheffield Lyceum seasons, Mr Hanson decided that in the next play, 'Double Door', I should play the Juv. Lead. "Do you good", he said "Good experience, 'stead of all these noses and things". Next Monday night I went on for the first house duly made–up, as I thought, as a typical Juv. Lead – 5/9 eye shadow, well shaped lips, little red dot in the eye–corner etc. As I came off from the curtain call I heard that unmistakable H.H. voice. "Mister Bean, Mister Bean, – that make-up! Who the hell do you think you're trying to attract, the girls or the boys? Get it off. I want it 'rugged', more 'rugged'".

......

Dora Bryan with many costume changes as 'Amy' in 'Little Women' got mixed up with one change, Mr Hanson's only comment "Why has Dora got blue bloomers with a pink dress?".

.....

David Tomlinson says H.H. only saw him once, during rehearsal, and fired him before they'd even opened. The play? "You Never Can Tell".

.....

H.H. after interviewing a young lady hopeful for a job said, "Right, report to Tonypandy on Monday". She said, "Oh thank you Mr Hanson; which company is he with?"

.....

One artiste bitterly resented being 'told off' by H.H., unfairly as he thought. When nobody was looking he made an alteration to the large bill-board outside the theatre. When H.H. arrived he was greeted by the sign: 'Harry Hanson resents the Court Players'.

❏   Frank Fortescue

Known throughout the business as "Oppy" because of his incurable optimism, Frank H. Fortescue presented Rep Companies, in many theatres, throughout the country for over 30 years.

His theatrical experience began at 14 when he played men's parts in portable theatres, doing a different play every night. He starred as Le Loup in 'The Face at the Window', and by the time he was 22 he had toured all the principal drama theatres in England, Scotland, Ireland and Wales.

In 1914 he started his own touring rep with plays like 'The Black Mask', 'Under Two Flags', 'Trilby' and 'The Sorrows of Satan'. He played the male leads and his wife, Jennie Hayden, played the female leads.

After the 1914–18 war he was leading man in several shows for the Kimberleys, and then formed a partnership with Mrs. F. G. Kimberley in revues, pantomimes and touring dramas, such as 'Ruined Lives', 'Her Bridal Night' and 'Tatters'.

In 1927 he sent out an elaborate production of 'Maria Marten', for which the bookings were so big that he had to follow it with a second company, one running for fifteen months and the other for seven. He followed this with tours of 'Dick Turpin' and 'Uncle Tom's Cabin'.

It was in 1923 that he opened his first rep company at the Royalty, Barrow. In the first two years he had six companies running: at Chester, Leicester, Reading, Bordesley, Wolverhampton, and Grantham. At one time he was running sixteen seasons, in addition to revues and pantomimes.

The list of theatres where he presented successful companies of Fortescue Players is so formidable that it is impossible to mention more than a few. Some of them are the Grand, Walsall; the Opera House, Dudley; the Empire and the Royal, West Bromwich; The Hippodrome, Wednesbury; the Opera House, Kidderminster; the Empire, Rotherham; the Grand, Luton; the Royal Bristol; the Metropole, Manchester; the Hippodrome, Preston; the Hulme Hippodrome, Manchester (nine–and–a–half years); the Playhouse, Manchester (three years); the Hippodrome, Wigan; The Queen's, Dublin; the Royal, Sunderland, and the Granville, Walham Green.

As with H. Hanson, F. Fortescue was a purveyor of popular entertainment which pleased a considerable portion of the population and, in those pre-TV days, offered a pleasurable diversion from the monotony of much working life. Today they have a greater choice of 'entertainment' on the TV each week, with the occasional visit to the theatre.

One actor who started his career with Frank Fortescue was Arthur Lowe of 'Dad's Army' fame. He joined the company at the Hulme Hippodrome, Manchester, on a weekly, twice–nightly, basis. Joan Lowe, Arthur's widow (stage name Joan Cooper) told me that she met Arthur, in 1947, at the Hulme Hippodrome, Manchester. She started her stage career with Donald Wolfit, and later did some acting, and stage management, at the Arts Theatre with Alec Clunes. She remembers F. Fortescue (who cam from Birmingham) as being a good and kindly employer. "On one occasion" she recalled "when I was feeling ill, he sent me home each evening in a taxi."

Arthur did some acting, during the Second World War, when he was in the forces; and afterwards he felt that he would like to become an actor. His father, who worked on the old L.N.E.R. rail, managed to get him a job with F. Fortescue, doing twice nightly Weekly Rep. Joan said, "had it not been for the Weekly Rep Arthur would not have survived." In the early days he did some radio work, but most of the time he worked in Weekly Reps. He (they) moved to Hereford, working for a year with the Derek Salberg Rep. Co.; and also working for Reggie Salberg at Penge and Croydon. Joan said "Arthur was always grateful for his Weekly Rep experience, where he acquired the fine sense of timing so essential to comedy acting."

Colin Bean, who was with A. Lowe in the 'Dad's Army' productions, recalls the difficulties faced by a Fortescue company during the war in his home town of Wigan. He writes, "Another tit-bit concerning the Fortescue Company in Wigan, particularly during the war, is, of course, the difficulties they had to face week by week just to get the shows on. Staging problems must have been horrendous. Hardly any back–stage staff, and actors and actresses being called away for duty either in the Forces or Factory work. The company arrived with about six sets of scenery and they had to manage the season on this. Occasionally there might be a 'Special Attraction' with 'Special Scenery from Manchester' no less! Most weeks, however, the set was The Kitchen Set, The Dark Oak–Panel, or the Light Oak–Panel Sets. If needed a Posh Boudoir–type Set (Hotels, Upper Class Bedrooms, and once – by the addition of stencilled N^s at the top of each painted column – Napoleon's Palace in 'A Royal Divorce') The Garden Set, possibly a Country Lane Front Cloth, and the Hippodrome's own stock variety–comic's Street Scene Front Cloth. A Wall-Papered Room and (in line with a wartime trend) a painted Panelled & Stippled Set. Usually one all-purpose staircase and anything else which (presumably)

Manchester HQ could let them have. Furniture and dressings had to be begged, borrowed or acquired from local shops etc. Arthur C. Goff was quite a familiar figure on a Monday morning, going down King Street (pipe going like a factory chimney) with an old clock or a large vase in his arms. An old Beam & Plaster set served for any play which had anything to do with 'the Country' or farms. If the Beam & Plaster Set was in use one week, quite possibly 'Friday Night Only! Special Attraction' would see a hastily put–together version of one of the old melodramas. One year the company presented 'Rebecca' very successfully, the next year they put it on for 'Friday Night Only – By Special Request'. God help the poor cast that weren't in the previous year's production, the mind boggles now – but what a wealth of experience one gained from weekly rep."

❏ Rex Howard-Arundel

"Dear Rex,
It was a pleasure to have you with us. Thank you for all you bring and the joy of your presence.
All good wishes,

Michael"

No man – yet alone an eighty-four year old, who is still active and working in TV – could be more justly proud of the above appreciation of his work, by a director of distinction, namely Michael Elliot; who was Artistic Director at the Royal Exchange Theatre, Manchester, from its opening until his early death in 1984.

The occasion was a party given for him when he had to leave the cast of 'The Dresser', at the Queen's Theatre, London, to fulfil a prior engagement.

This, for me, was a production that had some 'wonderful moments' and which I preferred to the film version with Albert Finney. (I think my disappointment with the film version of 'Amadeus' may have been due to seeing a fine stage version earlier at the Bolton Octagon theatre).

I doubt if there is another living person whose theatrical experience has been so varied as that of Rex Howard-Arundel. He has been associated with musicals, pantomime, repertory (much of this Weekly Rep) and latterly TV; plus writing successful plays!

His theatrical career began when, during the first World War, he obtained a part in a musical comedy called 'My Lady Frail' produced by world famous impresario Robert Courtnidge, the father of Cicely Courtnidge.

He was then still at boarding school in Gloucester, and this engagement brought him to the Opera House, Buxton. In 1985 he was there again playing in the televising of J.B. Priestley's 'Lost Empires' with Sir L. Olivier.

He toured with various companies and was playing at the London Hippodrome before he was 21.

He managed to get the rights of 'Mr. Wu' and he opened at the Old Brixton Theatre. This ran for 12 weeks and he made £1,000 – a lot of money in the 20's!

The first repertory company he ran was at the Empire Theatre, Wrexham in 1932, and he then continued to present repertory, in many provincial theatres, reaching his heyday in 1947 at the Bedford Theatre, Camden Town. He ran 'Reps' in many of the twelve theatres owned by F. J. Butterworth, a well known theatre personality.

In 1950 he rented a disused cinema from the Canterbury Council, re-named it the 'Marlowe Theatre', in memory of Shakespeare's rival, and put in a repertory company. Such was the success that the Council built a new theatre on the site, retaining the name 'Marlowe Theatre'.

Recently Rex's career as actor-manager, was featured in a Thames Television documentary, narrated by the late Sir Anthony Quayle.

Talking to Rex one soon realised that his involvement with different theatre activities, e.g. musicals, pantomimes, and Rep., plus writing plays, could lead one to think that he attempted to do too much (which on occasions was probably true); but he embodies the important fact that if you are engaged in work that interests you, and gives you satisfaction, then working long hours is no hardship. The picture of Weekly Rep as hours of drudgery, that is sometimes projected, reminds me of the story of the old lag who was in prison for sexual offences, and who remarked "if they would only let me out for a long weekend, I could go down to Brighton and work it out of my system!"

I'm sure that we have all noticed that, after a good sleep, 'it' is back again the next day and, providing one is healthy, needing some control and, hopefully, a creative outlet. The same is true of personal energy. 'Energy' wrote William Blake "is Eternal Delight".

Undoubtedly, the demanding routine of Weekly Rep was exhausting for some, but many thrived on this, and Rex Howard-Arundel, whom I had the pleasure of interviewing at eighty-four, did not appear to have suffered any ill effects. Apart from his TV engagements he was converting one of his plays entitled 'A Headful of Murder' into a thriller!

His son Howard, working as Howard Arundel, is a freelance film director, so the family name will be carried on in the profession.

The tradition of summer holidays spent by the sea, which was the custom in the British Isles until people began flying off to the Costa this and that, saw the appearance of many seasonal Weekly Rep companies.

In some theatres the change of play took place on the Thursday evening, thus enabling holiday makers to see two plays in one week.

Other names, who presented Weekly Rep companies in one, or more, towns throughout the country include Arthur Brough (TV viewers will remember his as Mr Grainger in 'Are you being Served') who operated at the Lea's Pavilion, Folkestone, on a seasonal basis. In 1929 he introduced tea matinees, and continued to provide repertory entertainment for 40 years.

Anthea Holloway remembered playing there. She wrote "When I worked at Folkestone – the Lea's Pavilion – for Arthur Brough, they did tea matinees – three a week. The Council owned the concession for the teas. So Wednesday, Friday and Saturday alternate rows were taken out and tables put in and teas were served all through the performance. It was nothing to hear "Miss, Miss, can I have some more hot water", or "Will you have the pink cake or the chocolate one" – competing with the actors on the stage. The only good thing was we could have the unsold left–overs between the shows."

W. Armitage Owen who, for ten years managed the Manchester (Rusholme) Rep theatre, also had companies in the north of England and Wales.

Barry O'Brien [1893–1961] was mainly a producing manager responsible for touring shows from 1925 until his death in 1961. This was interspersed with the running of repertory seasons in many provincial towns including Eastbourne, Bournemouth, Southsea, Shanklin and Ryde.

Richard Burnett, and his wife Peggy Paige, founded Penguin Productions Ltd., playing at the De La War Pavilion, Bexhill on Sea, and the Devonshire Part Theatre, Eastbourne.

The Bexhill venture began in 1950; and in 1958 they were invited to provide a pantomime, and a three month repertory season to follow, at the Devonshire Park Theatre. They continued to provide entertainment of a high standard, for 26 years.

I am indebted to Barry St John Nevill, who was the drama and music critic of the Sunderland Echo before joining the Eastbourne Gazette in a similar capacity in 1964, for the following comment, "Miss Page was still playing principal boy in their pantos aged 60 with much thigh slapping of very shapely legs. My vivid memory of them is of very charming people; content; not at all disappointed that they were not in the West End. For what they were doing, they were doing very well indeed, within tight budgets, and more important, they were delighting audiences of (mainly) rich people who had travelled the world, and who had seen a great deal of theatre. It says much for the high standards of the Penguin Players that they were able to please such discerning audiences."

T. C. Williamson and G. Lawrence combined to form the Lawrence–Williamson Rep Co., in the thirties, and played mainly in northern towns. In 1940 they played a season at the Bolton Hippodrome (reconverted from a cinema) and this lasted until 1959.

Towards the end of the long period of the Weekly Reps., Brian and Derek Pollitt, with his wife, founded the Galleon Theatre Co., in 1955, and they continued, mainly on a seasonal basis, providing entertainment at resorts in North Wales until 1965.

There were other names: all impresarios offering a 'mixed bag' of entertaining plays. Some made a profit and ended their days in relative comfort. Others ended with very little money and their state pensions. The money gained by one enterprise could soon be lost by the following one.

---

[1] P. N. Furbank's 'Unholy Pleasure' (Oxford 1985) is an interesting discussion of meaningful class terminology.

[2] Mary Kinloch Parker celebrated her 100th birthday in September 1990.

Chapter 20

Playgoers

"You became part of peoples' lives - public property. When my wife gave birth to our daughter in 1936 we were at St Annes and I had a cot handed over the footlights to me for her. People used to give us extraordinary presents at the end of our seasons. My wife was given a rosary once which belonged to the giver's dead brother but it was the only valuable thing she possessed and she wanted my wife to have it. During the war we had to stop if the siren went and ask any who wanted to leave to do so before picking up the scene where we had stopped – people who did leave often apologised for going but 'Mum is by herself' – or 'Dad's on warden duty and I've got to see if he is alright'."

G. Wood

"My friend and I used to go backstage to give the actresses flowers and chocolates and we used to be so thrilled when they had these gifts handed to them at the end of the performance. We were as dotty over meeting them as the youngsters are today over their pop idols, and when Christian Milne Thompson died, I wanted to die too, I nearly had a nervous breakdown, she was a lovely young girl".

A Leicester Correspondent

Rowell & Jackson's [1984] brief comment on the Weekly Reps is indicative of the mistaken nature of the composition of the audiences. They state 'Clearly the audience for a company with a weekly change of programme differed greatly from that for a theatre which offered a three week's or month's run'; and they also state 'The audience for Weekly Rep was inevitably smaller' – no evidence is offered for this extraordinary assertion! The number of Reps playing for more than a week could be counted on one hand between the wars. Not far from the old Birmingham Rep in Station Street – seating capacity of 450 – there is the Alexandra Theatre – seating capacity 1,500; and at the Grand Theatre, Wolverhampton, the seating capacity was 1,200. The former was weekly from 1927-43, and the latter from 1936-66. Though the fortunes of both varied (as did that at the Birmingham Rep) the combined attendances at these two theatres would be far in excess of that at the Birmingham Rep.

The audiences, in most of the Weekly Reps, consisted of a social mix. John Bennett, who was a director at Northampton during the Weekly Rep period, said "The dress circle was occupied by solicitors and other professional people plus fairly wealthy tradesmen; and the gallery was occupied by young-sters – especially on Saturday – when they were looking for a night out they could afford. In between there would be people from all walks of life".

The historian Sir Arthur Bryant, was a regular at Northamp-ton, and we have seen that Professor Dover Wilson was a regular at the Lyceum, Edinburgh; along with the observation that Louis Macniece was not impressed with the offerings at Birmingham Rep.

It is relevant here to point out that T. S. Eliot, the Sitwell brothers, John Betjeman, amongst others, found pleasure in attending Music Hall performances. No one could have been more intensely serious than Ludwig Wittgenstein, who found relaxation in reading detective magazines, and in visits to the cinema to admire the artistry of Fred Astaire and the dancing of Carmen Miranda. To a friend, regarding a projected visit to London, he made a request for him to find a 'film without any intellectual pretensions'. The philosopher A. J. Ayer was a life-long supporter of Tottenham Hotspur football club; and it is said that some of his students, discovering that this was so, began attending these football games – perhaps missing the point that he found aesthetic pleasure in watching the display of football skills.

The two pages Rowell & Jackson [1984] devote specifically to Weekly Rep are indicative of the need for a better researched account. In fairness they are implicitly more generous to the Weekly Reps than is apparent in their specific reference.

They acknowledge the exceptional quality of Osborne Robin-son (even reproducing one of his designs); the work of Herbert Prentice, and Ronald Russell at Bristol, but the main tenure of their approach is that more time and money will guarantee a better end product.

A play, by its very name is something to be played – to be performed. It is this significant fact that is sometimes over-looked by academic students of drama. If one needed the discipline of mind that is necessary to get to grips with Aristotle, Kant, Heidegger or Wittgenstein, to understand a play in performance, then few would go to the theatre.

This is not to deny that highly intelligent people have written for the theatre, and that their work may illuminate philosophical themes; but seeing and hearing a performance means far more than just treating it as another literary effort.

It would certainly be more economical, in view of present theatre prices, to buy three or four paperback editions of plays and stay at home and read them; but the evidence is that they cry out to be interpreted in visual and audible terms.

J. B. Priestley was quite uncompromising on this matter; "Anybody in search of pure thought will be well advised not to sit in a building with a thousand other people, a large company of actors, and an orchestra; better find a quiet corner at home and read a few books. . . . Nobody in his senses goes to the theatre to be told what to think".

Certainly in the early pioneering days of the Weekly Reps there were considerable numbers of educated people involved in the work, or support of them and who expressed the desire that these Reps should present 'worthwhile plays'; but what constitutes a 'worthwhile play' is not a simple question for which there are definite answers.

Was 'The Bells' a worthwhile play? Who today could say who the author was? Tyrone Guthrie comments: "many very ordinary scripts have been turned into great theatre by the 'over and above' of the performer's art. Irving's performance of Mathias in the The Bells is a conspicuous instance. Who now remembers that the script was adapted from Erckmann-Chatrian by Leopold Lewis? The script is of no significance, Irving's performance of Mathias legendary."

'Charley's aunt' is still played and enjoyed for the visual impact of its knock-about comedy.

I like the essential 'theatricality' of the story of the two playgoers sitting up in the gallery of a theatre, and below them, on stage, two actors are holding forth in a positive and declamatory manner. Suddenly, one of the playgoers begins to clap, and to his friend's enquiry "What's he saying?" he replies "I don't know – but it sounds damn good!"

A Ben Travers, or Ray Cooney, farce must be seen in performance to appreciate the skill of its construction.

Weekly Reps were usually good in presenting farce (cynics may say that 'it was one big farce') and this was mainly due to the actors being geared to working in a quick and lively way, and also being familiar with each other's limitations and strengths.

Remembering that, in the early days, the theatre was the main source of entertainment, the weekly visit to the Rep was one of the highlights, and many had regular bookings of the same seats. L. Jowsey of York writes, "Before the York Rep started the Theatre Royal consisted of stalls and pit, ground floor, dress circle, upper circle and gallery; here there were no individual seats but bare wooden forms and, if a particular play was proving very popular and the house was getting full, the attendant up in the gallery used to try to persuade the audience to sit closer together to get more people in. (This latter statement refers to Repertory performance). To me, this period of my theatre going was the happiest of my life.

First Tuesday was reserved for the theatre and I always took my mother and cousin. Under the aegis of the new company the stalls and pit remained unaltered, as did the upper circle and the gallery but the old dress circle was changed and the first two rows were the dress circle and the four rear rows were renamed the circle, and were cheaper. I cannot clearly recall the original admission charges but I know that for at least a year up to September 1939 the theatre had a system of Block Booking and the permanent reservation of seats. I used to buy a book of twelve tickets for the circle at a cost of 15s 0d (or 75 pence) and had permanently booked seats – front row of the circle – centre gangway. A book lasted me four weeks and the cost was 1s 3d. For the casual theatregoer the cost each for the circle was 1s 6d. Being a true Yorkshireman it was only second nature to buy the tickets 12 at a time and save 3d on each."

There is evidence to show that when some of the Reps went over to fortnightly periods there was considerable opposition from members of the audience. What were they going to do on the night of the second week? For many it was more than just a visit to see a play – it was the meeting place of friends and relations who lived on the other side of town, or out in the country. Though brief, news could be conveyed, and, more importantly, there was the shared experience of mutual pleasure. After a hard day's work at home, or in office or factory, they could sit and have a good laugh (or cry) together. Dorothy Goddard, of Sheffield, comments, "While doing nursing training at the (formerly) City General Hospital several of us, according to our duty times, made regular visits to the theatre, usually sitting in the gallery, the seat prices being within our limited budget. I have found an old autograph book containing some signatures of members of the repertory company whom we came to know from a distance and regarded almost as personal acquaintances. It gave us a sense of continuity to see these plays, one of the precious leisure activities we looked forward to during those years."

Comparing productions, during the period between 1915 and 1965, with the relatively few seen today in provincial subsidised theatres, is an almost impossible task; but the significant fact that emerged from the correspondence received in answer to my request for 'memories and impressions' of 'their Rep' published in local papers, from Plymouth and Hastings to Dundee; was that not one remarked about how much better productions are today compared with thirty, forty or even fifty years ago. I am, of course, referring to those who still go to the theatre, and for many the Weekly Reps were their first taste of this. Lala Lloyd recalls, "As far as human interest is concerned, I'd like to tell you of something that happened recently. I was at Waterloo on my way to the National Theatre – a woman asked the way there, said she'd come up from Kent. "What part of Kent" I asked – Sheerness, she said. "I know it" I said. "I know" she said "you were in Rep there, I went every week, it was the high spot of our lives, I've loved the theatre ever since – I recognised your voice at once". This was in 1983 and I was at Sheerness as you see in 1936. Very warming – and humbling."

I am sure that we have all had the experience of being afraid to admit to not being very impressed with this or that art manifestation which has been the subject of praise by some professional critics. Conversely, we may have enjoyed something which they regard as being of little importance.

In one sense, of course, it is possible to develop a discourse of great length starting from a seemingly insignificant object, or event.

One hears of the Oxbridge don, for example, who devotes a life time to a comma in a sonnet by Keats.

A large canvas, covered evenly with red paint, and with a white splash to be seen on its surface, may evoke seemingly endless speculation on the part of some art critics contemplating this modern artifact.

It matters not whether the white splash was placed there by the artist or; having been left exposed for a few minutes outside of the gallery, before being placed in position; a passing bird dropped a 'load' onto the canvas because it thought that, nature abhorring a vacuum, this would add to its artistic merit.

Discovering that this was in fact the case, would our assessors be mollified? Certainly not. They would find significance in this and continue their discourse.

Wittgenstein's statement that 'Philosophy is a battle against the bewitchment of our intelligence by means of language' seems appropriate here; though the rejoinder may well be 'Yes – but the battle can only be fought by means of language'. His further comment that what expresses itself in language, we cannot express by means of language, seems pertinent. We must recognise the linguistic boundary. We not only hear, we also see, the actors speaking the words, plus gestures, pauses, looks, and general physical movements; all of which add to the felt response to the play. Speculatively, I suggest that the theatre, in one sense, illustrates another main contention of Wittgenstein ...that certain things can only be shown and not said. This seems obviously true in play-dramas; but it is also there in the performances of Ken Dodd, Frankie Howerd, Max Wall, Joyce Grenfell, Victoria Wood, and other Variety and Music Hall artists.

Whilst some of the Weekly Rep playgoers would be aware of critical evaluations of the plays, the majority would not. They went to see a play, and they reacted in an open and honest manner.

If they enjoyed the play, as Joseph Walker indicated, it was apparent on their faces, and vice versa.

Undoubtedly, one of the main attractions of the Weekly Reps was that of being able to see the same actor in a different role each week.

An Edinburgh correspondent wrote, "One developed a habit of going because, I think, of seeing the same actors doing very different parts – the juvenile lead one week and an elderly part bit the next".

Chapter 21

From the 'Prompt Corner'

"One last thing, Mr. Mailes . . ."

"One last thing, Mr. Mailes. I'll ask you not to put the chamber under the bed, as the steam raises and rusts the springs."

Eric Barker, who joined the Birmingham Repertory company in the thirties, recalls this request being made by the landlady of the digs where Bernard Miles (now Lord Miles) was staying. 'Digs' have always been part of the life of theatre people, whether that was concerned with straight plays, opera, or variety and music hall; and, like many other aspects of theatre life, they differed considerably.

The dig most often mentioned is 'the comfy combine', which today would be similar to a bed-sit (minus the chamber pot under the bed!); and these were to be found during the period between the wars, and just after the Second World War.

During this period the division of 'legitimate' and 'illegitimate', or 'straight plays' and 'variety', was much more pronounced than in later years. Though in 1952, when I was engaged as the scenic artist, with a seasonal Weekly Rep company, at the Empire theatre, Dewsbury, following a season of variety entertainment, I was asked by the manager if I would like to stay on and help with the 'props' for the forthcoming pantomime. As there was little prospect of my obtaining work immediately before Christmas I agreed; and I distinctly remember one of the performers arriving one morning and complaining about his landlady... "snooty old bugger – she says she only usually takes Rep actors but will have me as long as I behave myself!"

In this pantomime there appeared two young men who, ironically, were later to do much to almost reverse this evaluation, namely Morecambe and Wise.

In recent years it would appear that the highest accolade an actor could wish for was, not to perform at the National, or with the R.S.C., but to appear on the Morecambe and Wise TV show!

This pantomime ran for about fifteen weeks and I remember

Eric and Ernie, not only for the maturing comedy talent they displayed then (they made their first entrance each kneeling in a pair of boots – the backs of which had been cut away – and each carrying a large suitcase so that their legs could not be seen, and evoking the comment from some members of the audience – "oh! I didn't know they were dwarfs!") – but also because, at the end of the run, they came, and thanked me, and gave me one pound! Almost nothing today but then a fifth of my weekly salary.

One of the biggest laughs during the run of this pantomime was not due to a part of the usual basic routine, but to a combination of circumstances that could not have been foreseen. It was customary at that time for the scene-shifters to be part-timers: men who did a job by day and came to the theatre in the evening to earn a little extra cash. If one was ill he would send a replacement; or the manager had a reserve list. This happened one evening and I remember the stage manager instructing the new man – rather small in stature – as to what he had to do at the end of the school scene. "The lights will go down and you then go on and collect the blackboard off the easel and place it at the back of the stage." The school scene began, and our new scene-shifter took up his position behind a large wing flat; rather like a long distance runner ready for the 'off'. What the stage manager had forgotten was that the lights also went down a few minutes before the end of the scene! This happened and our scene-shifting Sebastian Coe was on the stage in a flash – and in full view of about 1,500 members of the audience, took the blackboard off the easel and off stage. I can hear Eric's voice now as if it was yesterday – "I didn't know the bailiffs were due in!"

During the Weekly Rep season there, when I was painting the set, another young man would occasionally come and have a chat about 'Art" – sometimes carrying one of the Phaidon press publications on famous artistes (price £1.00). His name was Anthony Newley.

The impresario, who was responsible for the entertainment at this theatre, engaged a number of actors who had either achieved some recognition but were having a lean time, or who, like the veteran actor A. E. Matthews, were still glad of a fortnight's work. They would be paid a definite sum plus 5% of the week's takings. Anthony Newley had been seen as the Artful

Dodger in Oliver Twist, with Alec Guinness playing the part of Fagin. Later he was to join the cast of 'Cranks' and this was the beginning of a successful career. Others included Dinah Sheridan, Mai Zetterling and Robert Beatty. It was at this time that A. E. Matthews made the remark, "I get up in the morning – look through the obituary notices in the 'Times' and, if my name is not there, go off to rehearsals!"

Lala Lloyd, writing of 'digs' in the thirties says, "They were splendid. In working class districts. "Ma" looked after us – often she'd be up early to see her miner or similar jobbed husband off, then would light the fire in our room and bring breakfast, generally to our bedsitting room, known as a "comfy combined" – loo outside of course. I preferred self-catering which meant I bought the food and she cooked it – always supper ready when we got back from the theatre. Digs cost between £1 and £1.50 – the last almost 'star' digs. I used generally to pay £1.25 (all this in old money)".

John Haerem had a varied experience of digs in England and Ireland, where he was with the legendary Anew McMaster Shakespearian Co. [1939-41]. Of Ireland it should be noted that he says 'some of', "I always lived in digs. My first were in Macclesfield, My salary was £2 per week. I had a pleasant bed sitting room with coal fires, three cooked meals a day, as many baths as I wanted. Full cost 24s 0d (120 pence today). Some of the digs in Eire were appalling. No sanitation, poor food, dirty, and often one was covered in flea bites. Often kind landladies, and members of the public would present actors with practical presents of food, cigarettes etc. Especially Macclesfield."

Alec McCowen recalls his experience of landladies at York in 'Young Gemini'. He writes, "Theatrical landladies have almost disappeared. Nowadays, with frozen foods and laundrettes, young actors can look after themselves. But my days in rep are coloured by the many bedsitters I ate and slept in, and the many ebullient landladies who looked after me.

At first I lived with Mrs Meadows and then I moved to Mrs Lythe. Annie Lythe was a superb vivacious Yorkshire woman, and, in addition to looking after the lodgers and her own family, she was free for midwifery and laying out the dead. At lunch she would bring in crisp Yorkshire pudding with succulent onion gravy as a starter, and tell me details of her latest birth or death. Her little home was renowned as a great theatrical boarding house. Emlyn Williams always stayed in her first floor front, and I was often told, when she brought in my breakfast, that I had slept in Phyllis Calvert's bed – 'So you've got something to live up to!' She came to the first night every Monday and gave me notes before I went to bed. Once, after I thought that I had given a wonderful performance, she said: 'Well, you made a proper fool of yourself tonight!' The director confirmed this in the morning."

Today, in the Repertory theatres, there are few actors who remain for long with a company, and the theatrical landladies who catered for the professional actors, and whose conditions of service, and expectations of what they regarded as 'correct behaviour' varied – are almost extinct.

"Clothes - we provided our own . . . . . ."

"Clothes - we provided our own. My first job at Northampton taught me as much about dressmaking as it did about acting" wrote Lala Lloyd. "The men were expected to provide two lounge suits, dinner jacket, morning dress, casual clothes, hopefully, in those days, plus fours."

The provision of suitable clothing, to accord with the sartorial requirements of the character being portrayed, was met in varying ways by the many Weekly Rep companies.

Clothing for modern plays was provided by the actors themselves and, it would seem, the male members of the company fared better than the female. Diane Glyn comments, "Sunday, women were often at theatre ironing and preparing their wardrobes. Often we would have five or six changes of costume all provided by US (unless Period) and nothing could be worn again in a different play. I provided 20 full length evening dresses – 30 odd "smart" afternoon and cocktail dresses – had a dozen coats and skirts – negligees – stage undies – shoes. Men were much luckier (although they got paid more) their evening and dinner dress were (are) uniform – women's are different every time."

This is confirmed by Janet Burnell (Coventry 1935-36) and, as she was employed as a leading lady, which meant playing four lengthy parts out of five, it seems remarkable that she could find the time to design and make some of her own dresses. She writes, "It must be remembered that actresses had to supply up to three changes and sometimes more per production of all modern plays. It was the age of sophisticated glamourous comedies, of Noel Coward and Ivor Novello, of Norman Hartnell and his contemporaries. 'Haute Couture' was a necessity. A few actresses could borrow from wealthy friends. In Coventry there was a local tailor, Forsyth Brs., and a dress shop who were very good at lending models taking a great interest and even altering garments to fit. Forsyth in particular I was eternally grateful to... but it would not be more than one garment a month possibly. My main and most successful source was to design and make myself. Time consuming but at least I was sure of the result and afterwards they went into the dress basket building up a wardrobe for the future. In those days there were chains of fantastic "materials only" shops... Wools, etc. at 2s. 0d a yard or so, if one had the expertise and could make the time, one could produce fabulous results for a very small outlay. I had a portable Wilcox & Gibbs chain-stitch sewing machine, of my mother's, which was invaluable."

The provision of costumes for a period play would be met mainly by hiring from an agency or by the company having a wardrobe department. This latter provision would be found more in the companies that had their own theatre and workshops, with some space for storage. Hiring was an expensive business and consequently few period plays would be attempted.

At Sheffield, Edith Outram who, like so many Repertory members, had been a member of Sir Frank Benson's Shakespearian company, designed the costumes for some of the Christmas productions. However, these had to be made, and she paid a generous tribute to one of the many back stage personnel without whom the company could not have carried on. She wrote, "The first task ever entrusted to me was the designing and contriving of costumes for the Coventry Nativity Play. It was then that I first met Miss Cryer, who had offered to help. I did not know then that she was a highly expert dressmaker, but I was tremendously impressed by her quick understanding of my sketchy designs, her knowledge of the exact amount of material required for any garment, and her unerring cut; nothing that could be done with scissors, needle and thread was impossible to her, from the alteration of an existing garment to the fashioning of an entirely new one. On more than one occasion a dress was made overnight when one sent by the Costumier was unsuitable. She gave generously of her time and skill and was devoted to the theatre and its work. For years she acted as wardrobe Mistress and served in many other, less rewarding, ways."

The situation at the Royal Theatre, Northampton, during the period when Tom Osborne Robinson was the designer, is described by Bryan Douglas, "Costume at the Royal was in the hands mainly of two people – Tom did all the designs – apart from the odd small production when one of his assistants would do them, and these people changed over the years. Tom also did all the buying of materials.

The wardrobe mistress was Emily Jackley who was here for about 25 years. She died last year [1985].

Tom would give her drawings – some were more elaborate than others – some were works of art in themselves. Members of the company in those days were so taken by them that they often persuaded Tom to let them have them as a souvenir. Emmy used to do all her work in a very small room under the stage – cut off from all fresh air and daylight – the 9' x 4' cutting table I made for her practically filling the room apart from her sewing machine and shelves of – shirts – collars – shoes etc.

We kept everything and naturally accumulated quite a stock of period costumes which we used to hire out to less fortunately staffed theatres. They were all so well made that many are still in stock – though the bulk of them were lost in a fire at one of our stores in the 60's."

"The leading man for a long time was E. Hamilton Jordan. . ."

"The leading man for a long time was E. Hamilton Jordan, who was a considerable dandy and regularly could be seen on St Peters gate, wearing his monocle, and being admired by the local shopgirls. The heavy man for a long time was called Riseley and I recall a fight scene between he and Jordan, in Bulldog Drummond, which went on for several minutes as they crashed stage furniture and seemed out to do each other damage. I wondered in fact whether they had had an off-stage quarrel."

I first met the name of E. Hamilton Jordan in a letter from

Frank Bruckshaw, who was a journalist with the Stockport Advertiser, and the Cheshire Daily Echo, before the 1939-45 war. He wrote, "At the Theatre Royal, Stockport, the stage was occupied for long seasons by the Denville Stock Company with Charlie Denville in charge. They played Maria Marten, Sweeney Todd, Bulldog Drummond, The speckled Band, Damaged Goods, and The Yellow Ticket, amongst many others."

His next appearance in my research is a few years on at the Grand Theatre, Byker. This is where Kenneth More met him, and to whom we owe a description of this character, who was one of the last of a kind, in his Autobiography "More or Less" (1978). It is to his eternal credit that he always remembered and described his experience at this theatre with considerable warmth and affection; and readers, who wish to know more, can refer to this book.

During his stay at this theatre Hamilton Jordan was sacked by Charlie Denville. Kenny had assumed that he was a man of some standing and would have a little money put by but, on the morning of his departure, he asked him for four shillings to buy a beer and a sandwich on the London train. In Kenneth More's own words, "When I went to the station to say goodbye, I never imagined I would see him again, but I did, many months later, in London. There used to be a pub, The Round House, in Wardour Street, much frequented by actors waiting for work. I saw him at the bar, still wearing his outmoded clothes, but now without socks beneath his spats. He explained to me that he was suffering from dropsy and could not bear the constriction of ordinary woollen socks around his ankles. He therefore wore a pair of his wife's silk stockings beneath his spats. At a glance, it seemed that he had bare feet beneath the spats.

Years after this final brief meeting, I casually mentioned this story during a newspaper interview, and thought nothing more about it. At the time, I was making the film, The Admirable Crichton, and we were in the studios preparing one of the major scenes. Just as we were about to shoot, with dozens of extras clustered round, I became aware of one of these extras, a middle-aged woman, forcing her way through the crowd towards me.

She came right up to me, as I began to play the scene, and suddenly slapped my face hard on both sides.

'My God!' I cried. "What have I done? What's the matter?'

Everyone crowded round, wondering what had happened. She stood in the middle, a lonely, wretched figure.

'How dare you talk about my husband like that?' she burst out, almost in tears. 'He could always afford a pair of socks.'

Then she turned and ran away, weeping. She was E. Hamilton Jordan's wife. I had never met her before, and I never saw her again, but her proud loyalty to her husband's memory nearly broke my heart."

The photograph, dated 1927, shows him, complete with monocle, as a young man, with an Alfred Denville company, in Macclesfield.

Mrs Hamilton-Jordan died, at the Denville Hall, in March, 1985.

"In New Brighton there was a doctor . . ."

"In New Brighton there was a doctor who was a marvellous caricaturist – he used to watch the dress rehearsal if he could

Illustration 21.1 E. Hamilton Jordan

and then sketch the artistes with relevant pieces of action – this went to a printer and was at the front of the theatre by Monday evening – Tuesday morning at the latest. A marvellous man." (G. Wood).

Indeed!

The following note is taken from a York Theatre Royal programme of 1938, and indicates that professional people enjoyed their Rep visits, along with the other nine to ten thousand citizens of York who attended each week.

"Will doctors and other professional people, who are likely to have urgent telephone calls during the performance, please leave the number of their seat at the Box Office so that they can easily be found in case of emergency."

"The Welsh Players, started by . . ."

"The Welsh Players, started by a most extraordinary guy called Arnold Taylor, alias Robert Thornley alias... I can't remember. The fascinating thing about him was his exploits in Hollywood. Cecil B De Mille was making an epic pre-war. Arnold was on his production staff. There were elephants. They were mislaid. A few days later Arnold said he would find them and turned up next day with the elephants.... and got the reward. Of course, Arnold had taken them..."

I owe that story to Kenneth Vaughan, who was involved with Weekly Rep for many years. I'm sure that Damon Runyon would have enjoyed making that 'incident' a centre piece of one of his stories!

The precarious existence of the actors in Rep., and other theatrical enterprises, often led them to adopt various ruses to avoid Income Tax demands – "Try the Empire Theatre, Belfast" was written on one such request, and returned to the Inland Revenue office.

"Now you lot. . ."

"Now you lot, he shouted. 'If you have any aspirations to be actors and actresses, this is how it starts.' Whereupon he launched into what seemed an endless spiel about what it takes to be in the business and how to get there. I could contain myself no longer. Shrugging off Marilyn's restraining arm, I stepped forward.

'One moment please. I understand there to be another place where actors and actresses learn their craft. It is called repertory theatre. It teaches artists their business. I mean, not playing about like this. And if you took the trouble to ask, you would find that is where many of the people in this crowd have been for the last few years.'

'What's your name?' he demanded.

I told him. He wrote it down carefully. Marilyn was saying: 'Oh heck, you've done it again. You'll be out now.'

We were rounded up on the set and Preminger said to the assistant: 'Find me an interesting face or two for the close-up.'

The only name he had on his board was Patricia Pilkington.

'Miss Pilkington and her friend come out here, please,' he called.

And so Marilyn and I found ourselves under the scrutiny of the great Otto Preminger.

Our pixie hooded faces in close-up filled the screen for some seconds as St. Joan is burned at the stake. What cannot be seen is my torn dress. Marilyn trod on it, the skirt ripped away at the back and I was left shouting 'burn the witch' in, once again, nothing but my cami-knickers. Fortunately the shot was waist level."

This spirited defence of repertory theatre actors was made by the late Pat Phoenix (then Patricia Pilkington) who became Elsie Tanner of 'Coronation Street'. Pat spent a considerable number of years in Weekly Rep companies; all of which she describes in her book, 'All My Burning Bridges' [1974].

I doubt if more than a few of the customers entering the shop, selling electrical domestic appliances, in the village of Bramhall, in Cheshire, would know that, in 1952 theatre-goers on that same site were entering the Tudor theatre to see an actor and actress playing together who were to become two of television's most popular entertainers, namely Pat Phoenix and Ronnie Barker.

"I remember speaking with actors. . ."

"I remember speaking with actors in the wholly subsidised company in Finland during an Old Vic Scandinavian tour and their expressions of deep dissatisfaction that advancement (and lack of it), was determined by bureaucracy, seniority, retirement, or death. Our free enterprise, chancy scrambling competition held great appeal for them."

This, somewhat unorthodox, view of the subsidised theatre abroad is expressed by Leo McKern in 'Just Resting' [1984].

The whole business of the public funding of the Arts has given rise to considerable debate in recent years.

Ivor Brown in his book 'Old and Young', [1971] where he surveyed a long association with the theatre, states "In the opinion of one party the extent of help should be based upon excellence of performance. These perfectionists, centred mainly in London, insist that if they are doing their job well they should be helped to do it better still. They assume that the more public money is spent the finer performance will the public get. This may be true sometimes but it is often sadly false. I have seen theatrical productions, especially of Shakespeare, presented by highly endowed companies with such incompetence that any hard-up, over-worked remote repertory company would have been ashamed of them.

I meet general suspicion of wasteful expenditure by those who have the money to squander. Frequent purchase of new and unnecessary costumes is mentioned. So are the numbers on the payroll and the spate of new productions rashly chosen. Why 'make do and mend' if the taxpayer can be touched for another forced contribution?"

"Eight years after the war in a taxi in Chicago..."

"Eight years after the war in a taxi in Chicago, the driver said, "Are you English, then do you know Colchester and the Horse and Groom?" Yes, I was in the Colchester Rep". "Say, we've got to have a drink on this, I was stationed there and went to the Rep every week." I stopped, and he did take me out to a drink, and had a long nostalgic talk."

Joan Kemp-Welch, whom we met in my account of the Wilson Barrett company, recalls the above incident. In view of her long experience of working in the theatre and television, her comments on Colchester, and Weekly Rep in general, are significant.

"Robert Digby was another great theatrical character. To have worked at Colchester was like belonging to a club. I was there during the war years. Robert Digby put on a fantastic selection of plays – Ibsen, Chekhov, Shaw, Wilde O'Neil, Auden, Isherwood, Shakespeare, as well as new plays, American plays, revues, farces. He too lived for the theatre. Looking back it is incredible how we worked and what fun we had. In the summer we would often rehearse in someone's garden. Monday we opened the new play, Tuesday rehearsed Act 1 of the next, Wednesday Act 2 and Act 1 with words, Thursday Act 3 and Act 2 with words, Friday Acts 1, 2, and 3. Saturday run through play – matinee and evening show. Sunday we struck one set, built and let the next, Monday dress rehearsal and opening night and so on. After the first night of a play on Monday we would all go out together – Bob, stage management, cast, stage hands, either to the famous local pub – the Horse & Groom, known to every RAF and American Airforce personnel. Sometimes Bob Digby would get cars and take the whole company down to the sea, where he would produce drinks and sandwiches, and we would sit on the sand and put the theatre and the world to rights. Halcyon days, we celebrated VE night there and danced in the streets.

I acted in Weekly Rep at Northampton playing leads – long parts to learn every week and in my contract I had to provide my own clothes and a new frock each week. So my most vivid recollection was trying to learn lines and sew at the same time!

I was there at the same time as Stringer Davis, Noel Howlet, Sonia Dresdel. We used to play hard there as well; boating on the river every Sunday. I remember the lovely sets of Robinson – he was a genius. Weekly Rep and working with the same group of actors for a season, and playing different parts each week, was exhilarating, and I think the standard was every bit as good as today with two and three and even four weeks of rehearsal – but then we worked in those days. Fifteen pounds was a big salary in Weekly Rep and there were no hours set down and double pay for overtime. We just worked till the job was right, and we did have fun – I am sorry for the youngsters of today that this kind of experience is no longer available – it was worth its weight in gold."

Conclusion

There is no one kind of theatre, and no one solution to all its problems. That platitude needs to be repeated. The theatre exists by compromise, and feeds on contradiction. It exists to explain life, and to deny it, to decorate it and to strip it bare. Man goes to the play to understand himself, God or his neighbours, but he also goes to pass the time. He goes for uplift and amusement, a bit of fun and a moment of catharsis. The theatre is a weapon, a magic, a science; a sedative, an aphrodisiac, a communion service; a holiday and an assize, a dress rehearsal of the here and now and a dream in action.

R. Findlater

Some of the critics of Weekly Rep remind one of the athlete who, unable to run a mile in four minutes himself, declares that no one else can.

I hope that I have shown that a considerable number of Weekly Rep companies were the equivalent of four minute milers. With consistent effort, and discipline, a good performance could be achieved, and wonderful moments experienced by the audiences.

The ignorance (being unaware) of what had been happening in many provincial theatres for 30 years, including the few non-weekly ones, is nowhere better shown than in the remark of Irving Wardle, The Times drama critic, regarding the work of George Devine at the Royal Court theatre during 1956. He wrote "Devine's method of running his theatre with a small technical and artistic team was then new to Britain . . . . he had done all of the jobs himself. He knew what it was to put on a thimble and stitch all night; and he knew what could be expected of people and when the reasonable limits had been reached."[1]

That some became cramped and exhausted is not denied; 'time and chance' played a big part in the fortunes of individuals and companies.

180

In one sense, only those who have been really hungry appreciate what it means to have regular meals. One feels that many of the personnel working in the theatre today, where subsidy enables companies to have longer periods for rehearsals, now take this for granted and moans and grumbles are heard– and some seem to want, what in reality no one, at any time, has been able to guarantee future generations, assurances that conditions will be maintained at a certain level.

This is of course not peculiar to theatre only. In other areas, such as mining for example, I'm sure that the fathers of present day miners, who worked in the pits in the twenties and thirties, would find today's conditions of work luxurious compared with those in their working lives.

The important additional factor for the working actors, and this was especially true of the Weekly Rep ones, was that, at the end of his, or her, day, there was an applauding audience. The workers in offices, factories, mines, etc., finished each day with a mixed degree of work satisfaction; they certainly did not go home with the sound of applause still ringing in their ears.

The criticism that Weekly Reps did only plays that had been popular in West End theatres is again an oversimplification. Today, some of the provincial Repertory theatres now have studio theatres where some new plays can be performed, but the problem of what is a worthwhile play is still a difficult one.

J. C. Trewin remarked on the plays presented at the Plymouth Repertory, "Looking back, the programmes were fantastic; Shaw, Pinero, Barrie, Jones, Galsworthy, Maughan, Milne, intermingled with all kinds of popular pieces."

I have stressed that comedies vary in their structure and content, but even an agreed poor example may offer valuable acting experience. Rex Pogson, in his 'Miss Horniman and the Gaiety Theatre, Manchester' [1952] quotes J. Agate on Mona Limerick, an actress with the company at that theatre. "In a part calling for primitive emotion such as Nan she was overwhelming, a veritable tornado; critics could not find adequate praise for her. Other critics suspected from the first that outside such a part she could do nothing. James Agate, who saw her during these first weeks, summed her up in a piece of criticism which is at once a good example of Agate's uncanny rightness about acting and of the irritating (or endearing) showmanship he never lost. After assuring the actress that his only desire was to be helpful by pointing out technical short-comings he says, "Miss Limerick can look after the pounds well enough, she is careless of the pence. She can throw herself into French's arms with the obvious giving up of every nerve and fibre of her being, but she has not the least idea how to put her hands over her eyes in the previous scene. She had no comedy," he continued, and "one feels she has not played sufficient rubbish, the sort of stuff that has got nothing to do with the actor's brain but that provides exercises for correct breathing, the pronunciation of words like glad, match, etc., without any broadening of the vowel and builds up a proficient technique from the beginning. If only she could obtain variety and be persuaded to play a few stupid unimportant parts for a little time, he ended, she might have a great career before her."

Ray Cooney stresses the fact that in Weekly Rep the actor was often obliged to tackle parts for which he, or she, was unsuited; but this 'miscasting' was something one also could learn from. He comments "It is interesting to note that so many popular playwrights of the period between 1950 and 1970 were actors who were the product of Weekly Rep companies. I believe the reason for this is that we were steeped in the 'theatre'. We lived it and worked it 24 hours a day. We did nothing but talk about plays – their construction and the effect of them on our audience; why some plays worked and some didn't."

Kenneth Watson wrote: "One thing which Weekly Rep did teach supremely well and which appears so deficient in many so-called comedy actors of today, was timing. It's hell-hard for a light comedy actor to time a laugh to a camera, even with a studio audience. To your experienced Weekly Rep actor of 45 years ago it was second nature. If he didn't learn the trick he wouldn't last long in any company. Other things he learnt which your young actor today has far less opportunity to learn, are presence of mind – how to gag his way out of an awkward spot, like someone being off by a mile, or a door handle suddenly coming off in his hand."

The late Rex Harrison, in a TV programme about himself, commented about the difficult task of playing in light comedy, quoting a remark attributed to David Garrick "Any fool can play in tragedy - comedy is a damn serious business". Simon Callow, reviewing a book on Rex Harrison[2] made the following comment on light comedy "Practitioners of this brutally demanding art cannot confine themselves to their own part; no comedian is an island. Light comedy, too, has the special onus of needing to be perfect. The culinary metaphor applies here exactly: a soufflé that doesn't rise isn't a soufflé at all".

I doubt if the critics would agree as to what constitutes 'perfection' in this area; but the excellence of much of the light comedy acting in Weekly Reps. was due to the fact, stressed by Reggie Salberg and Ronald Russell, of experienced actors playing together for long periods.

There are certainly more plays being written today than ever before, and there is little likelihood of them being performed; so a literary judgement has to be made, though one assumes that an experienced producer (director) will be able to judge the 'theatrical' potential of a play. Undoubtedly, for the playwright, as with the actors, 'time and chance' play a big part in his, or her, development.

The number of new plays seen on TV, and heard on the radio, far out number those in the theatre, and since the number of theatres putting on straight plays is now about a fifth of the total before 1960, Weekly Rep has been replaced by weekly TV. Theatre going, which was once a habit is now an occasion, and the majority of the Reps are dependent on public funding from the Arts Council and local authorities.

In the main it comes to the consideration of the importance of theatre in a nations' life. Those who are the most vociferous in demanding public funding to keep theatre alive do tend at times to talk as if there was not any 'drama' being seen by the majority of non theatre goers, overlooking the fact that in any week the TV will offer good drama at least for the equivalent of theatre time, usually three to four hours.

The problem here is that along with the equivalent time one would spend in a theatre there is much that is of questionable value. During the long run of the Weekly Reps there was no 'pop culture' attracting so many young people, or TV.

Cynics have observed that in a democracy the village idiot can be voted onto the local Education Committee, and freedom of expression must see the appearance of much that is dogmatic, biased, vulgar, arrogant, ignorant, and superficial, besides work whose value is perhaps only discerned by a consistent minority.

Freedom implies the ability to be able to move backwards as

183

well as forward. In this century the biggest blow to the notion of 'inevitable progress' was delivered by Hitler. Some might add Stalin and Pol Pot. Those who believe that conditions can be established, that will set in motion an inevitable forward movement, can be compared to the working of a toy round-about on which there are models of human figures. Some of these fall over and the manipulator presses a button, the roundabout stops, and the figures are stood up again. Another press of the button and the roundabout continues. With human beings there is no outside manipulator to stop the world and adjust the figures. The figures have to be corrected whilst the roundabout of human history keeps turning – and only the figures on the roundabout can help, or hinder, each other.

Social theorists of any kind seem to, perhaps unconsciously, assume that the world can be stopped, things adjusted, and then set in motion again.

Historically, the world of each individual could always be abruptly ended. One of my favourite quotes (though I don't know its origin) is "if you were told that you were going to die in a month's time you would be very concerned – you laugh when you can't be sure that you will live another ten minutes!"

With nuclear devices not only can 'my world' be abruptly ended, but 'the world' can be destroyed. Logically, this may now be in ten minute's time, or less; but equally, the world of conscious human beings may still be functioning ten million years from now.

For some dramatists the world may seem a place "where but to think is to be full of sorrow and leaden-eyed despair" but though there is cruelty, violence, rape, poverty – there is also generosity, kindness, courage, and remarkable organisation of the creation, and distribution, of much of the world's re-sources.

After retiring from his position as the drama critic of the Sunday Times; Harold Hobson, reflecting on a long life of theatre going, concluded with the following remarks:

"In the theatre today there is too much talk of sex and not enough of love. There is an excessive preoccupation with homosexuality. The unjustified contempt for entertainment plays increases. There has been a continuous degeneration of language. Freedom of speech may be allowed, but freedom of thought is not. Finally, there has been an almost complete loss of what Aristotle held to be the chief mark of a dramatist – the capacity to construct a plot. All the causes – Beckett, Osborne, Pinter – for which I fought have been won, and there have been several brilliant achievements. Nevertheless, on the whole the result has been desolation. The battles will have to be fought all over again, and the other way round until it once more becomes possible on the stage for a young man to fall in love with a girl, or speak of his country without contempt, or for an audience once again fully to understand and share such tenderness and longing, such soaring exultation, as Robert Tear brought to the singing of Giuesppe Giordani's love song Caro mio ben ('without you my heart languishes') in Westminster Abbey on 17 November 1983, in a service of thanksgiving for the life and work of Sir Ralph Richardson, an actor so often mentioned with affection, admiration and gratitude in the preceding pages."

I believe that what distinguishes Shakespeare, Tolstoy, or Dickens, from other members of the human race is not that their experience was so different; but that they could give this such a remarkable structure; though when they attempt to give a structure to experience that they themselves have not had, e.g. the old age of King Lear; then we are in the domain of imaginative speculation, and the difficulty here is that there is no objective criteria of what counts as 'the same' in human experience.

I believe that we confuse 'the communication of experience' with 'the structuring of experience'.

Experience is something we have – we neither receive it or pass it on; but we do attempt to give it a structure through language and visual means, and drama is one of the most effective ways of doing this.

T. S. Eliot's remark that "humankind cannot bear too much reality". . . I believe to be true; that is why we go to a theatre, or a cinema, or sit comfortably in a chair at home watching TV or reading a novel. No matter how cleverly we may give the illusion of cruelty, rape, murder and mutilation (Titus Andronicus seems to be very much favoured) we know that the 'lived throughness' of the actuality is not being experienced. For anyone who thinks, for example, that no matter how good the acting, watching a portrayal of football hooligans' behaviour being portrayed in the theatre; and he or she thinking that they are experiencing the reality of the 'lived throughness' of the experience there is a simple cure. Sadly today, all they will have to do is to go to almost any football ground of one of the teams in the four divisions, stand amongst the home supporters and shout loudly for the visiting team.

It would be putting a poor price on life if we thought we could have another person's experience for the price of a theatre, or cinema ticket, or a TV licence, or a novel. God forbid that our theatre 'realists' should ever attempt 'Smellarama'!

I have said little about working conditions and trade union activities.

Because there have always been some bad employers (and here I include that amorphous, and shapeless one, called 'the State'), the only way to deal with these is by united action on the part of the oppressed. However, when these become the powerful manipulators themselves, their demands may be excessive and self defeating.

I believe that J. B. Priestley's picture of the 'two theatres' is still true. Some of the first may be financed, either by the Arts Council, or a private investor. I have no doubt that the second was to be found sometimes in the Weekly Reps; and today, more likely to be experienced in some of the 'fringe' theatre venues. Though here one feels that there are enthusiasts (including the graduates from University Drama Depts.) who mistake 'being different' for being 'truly original'. Plus the fact that there is little opportunity for them to acquire the acting skills which the Weekly Rep venues provided.

Though I doubt if the present graduates, assuming that Weekly Reps existed, would be willing to attempt working in this area. As Jonathan Miller notes "The university actor is often rather affected and arrogant. Many of them enter the theatre with a highly self-satisfied style of performance which is partly reinforced by their sense of themselves as graduates".[3]

I hope I have shown that the picture of exhausted actors, ad libbing and muddling through (and large numbers of the citizens of the many towns where this took took place willing to pay for this!) is, in the main , a concoction of ignorance.

I should be pleased, if in future, when Weekly Rep is mentioned, there is not the usual cursory dismissal of an activity that is not worthy of consideration; but that people will pause and consider the exceptional achievement of many talented and gifted artists.

How do I 'ring down the curtain' on my conclusion?

Perhaps with the comment of Reggie Salberg, "Weekly Rep was not a desirable state of affairs, of course, but some remarkable work was done. I don't know how we achieved those miracles."

Of course – what is a 'desirable state of affairs?' is still an open question. For the tens of thousands who attended the many theatres, housing Weekly Reps, between 1915-65 I will leave it to Mary Inglis who wrote to me from Edinburgh.

"I am coming up for 72 years and when I first started as a young girl to go to the Lyceum Theatre it was the "Macdonna" Players with Esmé Percy, then came the Jevan Brandon Thomas and finally the Wilson Barrett Company. At first my friends and I used to leave our office on a Tuesday evening and stand in the queue for "The Gods" admission 6d pence. We had to run up endless stairs to get a good seat near the front. Hard wooden seats with no backs – but we survived. Then we promoted ourselves to the Upper Circle for 1/3d, tip-up seats and backs. What a luxury! We had some wonderful nights and made many friends.

They were a wonderful company and had to work very hard indeed. Rehearsing for the following week while playing a different play in the evening. How they never got mixed up, shows what great stuff they were made of."

---

[1] From 'The Theatres of George Devine" [1978] Jonathan Cape.

[2] Rex Harrison: The First Biography by Roy Moseley [1987] Hodder.

[3] From 'Subsequent Performances' by Jonathan Miller [1986] Faber.

Bibliography

Acting in the Sixties: Edit. Hal Burton, BBC Publications (1971)

Agate, James: The Selective Ego (1976) Edit. by Tim Beaumont

Alexander, Jean: The Other Side of the Street (1989)

Appleyard, Bryan: The Culture Club (1984)

Barrett, Wilson: On Stage for Notes (1954)

Barker, Eric: 'Steady Barker' (1956)

Barker, Ronald: It's Hello From Him (1988)

Belfrage, Bruce: One Man in His Time (1951)

Bennett, Arnold: Literary Taste (1909)

Brambell, W: All Above Board (1976)

Boucher, R & W G Kemp: The Theatres in Perth (1975)

Brown, Ivor: The Way of My World (1954)

      Old and Young (1971)

Browne, Maurice: Too Late to Lament (1955)

Butler, Nicholas: Theatre in Colchester (1981)

Callow, Simon: Being an Actor (1984)

Campbell, Donald: A Brighter Sunshine (1983)

Cardus, Neville: Autobiography (1947)

Carter, James: Oldham Coliseum Theatre (1986)

Crane, Harvey: Playbill (1980)

Chisholm, Cecil: Repertory (1934)

Dyas, Aubrey: Adventure in Repertory (1948)

Elsom, John: Theatre Outside of London (1971)

Findlater, Richard: The Unholy Trade (1952)

Fraser, A K: The Alexander Theatre (1948)

Flynn, Erroll: My Wicked, Wicked Ways (1960)

Fothergill, John: An Inkeeper's Diary (1931)

Godfrey, Phillip: Backstage (1933)

Goorney, Howard: Theatre Workshop Story (1981)

Greaves, Jane: Oldham's Theatres (1976)

Guinness, Alec: Blessings in Disguise (1985)

Guthrie, Tyrone: A Life in the Theatre (1959)

Hartnoll, Phyllis: (Edit) The Oxford Companion to the Theatre (1983, 4th Edition)

Hayman, Ronald: The Set-Up (1973)
    British Theatre since 1955 (1979)
Hird, Thora: Scene and Hird (1976)
Hobson, Harold: Indirect Journey (1978)
    Theatre - A Personal View (1984)
Howe, P. P.: The Repertory Theatre (1910)
Hurren, Kenneth: Theatre Inside Out (1977)
Isaacs, W: Alfred Wareing (1951)
Kendal, G: The Shakespeare Wallah (1986)
Knowlson, Joyce: Red Plush and Guilt
Knight, Esmond: Seeking the Bubble (1943)
Leacroft, Helen & Richard: Development of the English Play-
house (1971) Pbk (1978)
    Theatre and Playhouse (1984)
    Theatres in Leicestershire (1986)
Marshall, Norman: The Other Theatre (1947)
McCowen, Alec: Young Gemini (1979)
McCoola, Ros: Theatre in the Hills (1984)
McGrath, John: A Good Night Out (1981)
McKern, Leo: Just Resting (1984)
More, Kenneth: More or Less (1978)
Mesurier, Le John: A Jobbing Actor (1984)
Nichols, Peter: Feeling Your Behind (1984)
Offord, John: The Theatres of Portsmouth (1983)
Payne, Ben Iden: Life in a Wooden O (1977)
Phoenix, Pat: All My Burning Bridges (1974)
Pick, John: The Theatre Industry (1985)
    Managing the Arts - The British Experience (1986)
    The Arts in a State (1988)
Pogson, Rex: Miss Horniman and the Gaiety Theatre (1952)
Priestley, J B: Theatre Outlook (1946)
    The Art of the Dramatist (1957)
Rix, Brian: My Farce from my Elbow (1975)
Rosenfeld, Sybil: The York Theatre Royal . . . to 1948
    Typescript in York Reference Library
Rowell, G & Jackson, A: The Repertory Movement (1984)
Russell, Ronald: The Story of the Little Theatre, Bristol (1948)
Salberg, Derek: My Love Affair with a Theatre
    A Mixed Bag (1984)
Sanderson, Michael: From Irving to Olivier (1984)
Seed, Alec: The Sheffield Repertory Theatre (1959)

Simonson, Lee: The Art of Scenic Design (1951)
    The Stage is Set (1932)
Sinden, Donald: A Touch of the Memoirs (1982)
Southern, Richard: Changeable Scenery
Trewin, John: Theatre since 1900 (1950)
    We'll Hear a Play (1949)
Tompkins, Peter: Shaw and Molly Tompkins (1961)
White, Michael: Empty Seats (1984)
Williams, Dorian: Master of One (1978)
Williamson, Audrey: Theatre of two Decades (1950)
Wyndham-Goldie, G: The Liverpool Repertory Theatre (1935)
Western Popular Theatre: (Edit) D Mayer & K Richards (1977)

Additional Sources

York Theatre Royal Souvenir Book, 1734-1984
Liverpool Playhouse Golden Jubilee, 1911-1961
The Redgrave Theatre, Farnham
Perth Theatre Anniversary, 1935-1985
Playhouse Souvenir Programme, Amersham, 1936-1946
The Stage and Television Today
Stage Year Books
Theatre World
Dobson's Theatre Year Book, 1948-49
Who's Who in the Theatre, 1912-77
Who Was Who in the Theatre, 1912-76 (4 Vols.)

Index

193